BRAMAN'S

INFORMATION ABOUT TEXAS.

CAREFULLY PREPARED

BY D. E. E. BRAMAN,

OF MATAGORDA, TEXAS.

PHILADELPHIA:

J. B. LIPPINCOTT & CO.

1858.

TO THE PUBLIC.

THIS little volume has been written solely for the benefit of persons seeking information about Texas, and the matters herein contained are definite and reliable. The author, within the last ten years, has received scores of letters from abroad, making inquiries about the soil, climate, and productions of the country, the land system, land claims, taxes, and all the other various questions which suggest themselves to minds stimulated by curiosity or interest; hence, the present volume. There are men and women, in every State in the Union, having interests in Texas, of one kind or another, to many of whom the information herein contained will be of vital importance. There are others, also, who would like to cast their future lots in this favored land; but they find it so difficult to get reliable information about the soil, climate, land system, and other important matters, that they hesitate, lest, when too late, they should rue the change. I have, therefore, endeavored to collect and collate all of those descriptions of practical knowledge which will be of most interest and benefit to such persons. I acknowledge myself under obligations, for valuable information, to those excellent journals, the "Galveston News" and "State Gazette," published at Austin; and further deponent saith not.

D. E. E. BRAMAN.

MATAGORDA, *Texas.*

CONTENTS.

CHAPTER I.

CHAPTER II.

CHAPTER III.

CHAPTER X.

CHAPTER XI.

CHAPTER XII.

CHAPTER XIII.

CHAPTER XIV.

CHAPTER XV.

CHAPTER XVI.

CHAPTER XVII.

CHAPTER XVIII.

CHAPTER XIX.

CHAPTER XX.

CHAPTER XXI.

CHAPTER XXII.

INFORMATION ABOUT TEXAS.

CHAPTER I.

INFORMATION FOR EMIGRANTS ABOUT DIFFERENT PORTIONS OF TEXAS.

THE middle and northern counties of the State are settling faster than those on the seaboard, and the tide of emigration, which is continually rolling in through Arkansas and Louisiana like a spring flood, will, in the course of three years, so change the face of nature, that strangers would not believe the results; to this conclusion are we brought, not by our desire for aggrandizement, but by what has transpired within the last like short period of time.

The emigration for the western and seaboard counties generally arrives by water, and is not so numerous or so regular; the foreigners seek the western counties, to commingle with their countrymen who fortunately came earlier.

I have, for convenience, divided the State by certain arbitrary designations, as follows, viz:

Northern counties, all above 32° of north latitude.

Middle counties, all above 31° and below 32°.

Interior counties, all above the seaboard counties and below 31°, and east of the Colorado River.

Western counties, all west of the Colorado and south of 31°.

Seaboard counties, all bordering on the Gulf of Mexico and on the connecting bays.

Emigrants owning ten slaves or upwards, and who desire to raise cotton or sugar, will find it most in accordance with their interests to select some of the fine alluvial soils of the seaboard counties, east of the Colorado. Emigrants intending to rely mainly on stock-raising, will find no better locations than on the edges of the large prairies that lie between the alluvial lands; in the aggregate they are vast, and inexhaustible in herbage.

Emigrants having negroes, but less than ten, can do well in any part of Texas; I think, however, the interior counties will suit their interests best, where the lands are more diversified in quality and character, with smaller and better prairies for cultivation, and more timber; where cotton, and all the grains and fruits flourish, and come to perfection; and where each planter or farmer can raise his own horses, mules, and cattle.

This region possesses advantages which allow of the combination or intermixture of farming, planting, and stock-raising, all together, or either one of those employments separately; but it is found most profitable and comfortable to accept all the boons of

Nature, and not to be confined to one calling or product exclusively.

The people are more rural and domestic, and less aristocratic than in the seaboard planting region. The farm or plantation is the home of the owner and his family, and those persons who possess slaves either labor with them, or superintend them personally; happiness, enjoyment, and independence, dwell among this people, and their few slaves are component parts of their families, and partake of the joys and sorrows of their protectors. All those portions of Middle and Interior Texas, lying on or near the Colorado, Brazos, Trinity, Sabine, and Neches rivers, and their tributaries, are very fertile, and quite densely timbered. The cotton planters who leave the seaboard settle here. Population is very generally diffused over the interior counties, and the cities, towns, public improvements, substantial private residences, snug farms and plantations, sleek cattle and horses, and the long trains of ox wagons going to and from the towns, laden with what the soil yields, or some equivalents, bespeak an easy independence among the people.

The eastern portion of Interior Texas was settled in early times; still there is plenty of good land for sale at low prices.

Middle Texas, west of the Trinity, was settled much more recently than the former, and is not, as a general thing, so desirable a country; nevertheless, the counties lying on the Trinity, and all west of it, have much excellent land; the further west we go the better the land becomes; and between the Brazos and Colorado they are equal to any portion of the State.

This region is much diversified, and contains many varieties of land, some of the very best quality, and much that is considered in Texas poor. Some large districts of timber, and again other parts where timber trees are a novelty; here the prairie lands are the best for cultivation, being easy of tillage, and very productive in wheat and all the cereals, but wheat seems to be the staple production. Of fruits, apples, pears, quinces, and plums, ripen to perfection. Industrious emigrants from the older States will better their conditions amazingly by seeking homes in Middle Texas. The climate is generally healthy; the winters are short, and colder than on the seaboard; the spring seasons mild, and glowing with budding life; and the summers are long, dry, and sultry; the autumns are pleasant and agreeable, neither too hot nor too cold, and frequently encroach much on winter's dominion.

Water from wells is always cool and wholesome, and the streams and springs are usually potable. Some, however, hold minerals in solution, or other deleterious matter, which requires the new-comer to be cautious.

Northern Texas is the region destined to become the most prosperous and thickly populated part of the State, and, although but recently recognised as being within habitable bounds, has already a large population.

I was told by some gentlemen, who recently travelled through Cook County, the most northern territory of the State, that they were scarce ever out of sight of settlements. Wheat was selling at fifty cents per bushel. This, it is true, is an evidence that the demand is not commensurate with the production, but it also shows a well adapted, productive soil, and the interest is becoming so important, that a demand will be created through the agency of railroads. There are no large rivers in this region; but it is well watered with brooks, rills, and streamlets, that incessantly flow, through all seasons.

The climate is exceedingly healthy, and the seasons are sufficiently marked by summer's heat and winter's cold, by the bland zephyrs of spring, and the still mellow autumnal days and frosty nights, to give a pleasing variety to the course of the year. To the industrious farmer, who has the health, will and independence to till the soil, this region offers superior advantages to all other parts of the State; here will be made the flour, butter, cheese, and salted meats for the large seaport towns; this is the Goshen, the land of promise of the Southern States. A thrifty farmer, now living in Cook County, and who has become rich, told me that he formerly lived in the best wheat portion of the State of New York, that he afterwards moved to Ohio, and from there to Illinois, but that he had never seen such excellent land for wheat, or so large crops, in any of those grain States, as in Cook County. The long distance of the northern counties from the seaboard, and the majority of them being far from any navigable stream, have prevented emigrants who came by water from getting so far inland, and the markets for productions being distant, and difficult of access, a proper stimulus for extensive and thorough cultivation of the soil is lacking. I have been credibly informed, that a man with a plough, drawn by one horse, may break up any of the tillable soil in Cook, Fannin, Denton, Grayson, and Lamar counties, so that he may plant wheat, corn, and potatoes, and that the two latter require very little after-cultivation. The prairie lands are always preferred, being easier to cultivate than the timber lands, and, in fact, are the only first-class soils.

The mode of travel, for emigrants to Middle and Northern Texas, is the same that was practised by the first emigrants from New England to Ohio and the Western States, across the Alleghenies: highly primitive, and suggestive of patience and long suffering.

Northern Texas is infected with none of the pestiferous miasmatic vapors which arise, in many, otherwise desirable, localities, from swamps, morasses, and stagnant ponds, and which are so fatal in many new States. The climate is healthy, and restorative to shattered constitutions. Nevertheless, emigrants should be careful, for a year or two, and not expose themselves unnecessarily to wet, cold, or hot sun: in the middle of the day, in summer, labor should be avoided: drink not the cold spring water when heated, be careful in diet, eat moderately, and of simple, well-cooked food, eschew whiskey and all other poisonous drinks, make daily ablutions of the entire body, when first out of bed, and keep your temper cool and your mind contented; and, if you are an honest man, a good husband and father, your health, under ordinary circumstances, will last to old age, and until the human machine shall have been worn out by lapse of time. I would also recommend that you keep on good terms with your wife, govern your household like a Christian, and be at peace with your neighbors: have a small library of select works, and subscribe to one or two good newspapers, so that your evenings and leisure hours may be spent profitably and agreeably, and yourself and family receive intelligence, and keep informed of the busily passing events of the old world.

Those emigrants who bring children should keep them out of the hot sun and inclement weather, feed them sparingly on simple food; no tea, or coffee, or other narcotic stimulants; and bathe daily. I place great confidence in the frequent outward use of cold water, as a preventive and curative; and contend, that accumulated dirt under the garments is just as offensive and filthy as a dirty face or hands, and a greater harbinger of ill-health. I do not make all these recommendations because I think there is any critical period or season here, called the acclimating; but I know that emigrants are deprived of many of the comforts which they enjoyed in their old homes; that they are necessarily subject to more exposure and privations; that the care and anxiety for their success, for the health and comfort of their families, the uncertainties and disquietudes about a problematical future, all conduce to unhealthy excitement, and disease; and, even in their native climate, under like mental and physical exertion, sickness would result. I can imagine what a destructive, trying, and expensive affliction sickness in an emigrant's family is; how it stops all the wheels of advancement, distracts the future plans and calculations, and swiftly eats away the humble substance. And then, if death come — how terrible and overwhelming! — the cot becomes desolate to the living, the beauties of the new home, the wild scenery, the domestic arrangements — all are turned into objects of loathing, the precincts of the charnel. I would further caution new-comers who desire peace, prosperity, and health, to avoid lawyers, doctors, and quack medicines, and all other unseemly monsters, and to attend strictly to their domestic affairs. Firstly, after arriving, if not before done, they should select a good tract of land; for, in a country like this, where there is so much for sale, a man should not be contented with any but of the first quality. It is best to have it fronting on a stream, if possible, where plenty of wood, for fencing and fuel, is handy; and, if meandered by creeks, brooks, or spring rills, it is all the more desirable. Let him select high ground for his dwelling, protected, at the north, by timber or irregularities in the land; let the house, in the improvements, be first built—an humble edifice will answer best: it should have a good floor and tight roof, *above* all. The house should stand on blocks of wood or stone, at least two feet above the ground, so that the fresh air may circulate freely: there should be no chance for water to accumulate under the dwelling, for an instant: all stagnant pools anywhere should be dispelled. After the human dwelling comes the cow-pen, made, in the most convenient mode, with strong rails and posts: then should be purchased a few good cows, according to means and advantages of prairie pasturage: then the animals for a team; oxen are preferred, for small farmers, as being less expensive, easier kept, and more readily obtained; and the farmer can, after three years, renew his team from his own stock, and turn out the old oxen to make beef, when they are no longer fit for work—they soon fatten on the prairies. Emigrants can always purchase lands in Texas on better terms than in any of the other States, for the reason that it was acquired from the sovereignty of the soil, by the original possessors, by free gift.

An emigrant should never purchase less, at first, than 320 acres of land: this can be acquired for a small advance in money, and the balance on long time—the purchaser giving his promissory note, with mortgage on the land.

After finding a suitable tract, and the owner

thereof, and entering into negotiations, the emigrant should have an examination, at the county clerk's office, to see if the coveted land is free from all incumbrances, and the title in the ostensible owner. Then resort to the district clerk's office, and see that there are no judgments against the owner; also ascertain if all taxes are paid; after which, he may conclude his purchase, always being sure to take a conveyance, with full covenants.

After the dwelling and cow-pen, the next labor is to select the richest soil out of the tract for cultivation, and plough enough for the first year's corn, wheat, potatoes, oats, millet, and minor vegetables. He should commence ploughing immediately after arranging a shelter for his family, and an enclosure for a few milch-cows. No matter what time he arrives, even in the summer, the ploughing, at that season, turns in the heavy coat of vegetation, which improves, lightens, and quickens the soil: another slight ploughing, in the fall, before sowing grains, conduces much to a good yield. The ploughing for corn and potatoes should be done in January, or the first of February. Planting may be done in the latter month, and along until the last of April. It is true that the soil very seldom gets more than one breaking up; and that, with this, good crops are raised, in ordinary seasons; but, if time can be spared, more husbandry will well remunerate the extra labor.

It is a momentous affair for a family, in the older

States, surrounded with the ties of relations and friends, with local attachments for home, and all its recollections and *heart*-ties, to bid good-bye forever; to take a long last look of places and friends, which affection, time, and long familiarity, have made too dear; to quit all these, and plunge into the great stream of emigration, which leads, the adventurer knows not whither, requires nerve; for it is a very serious matter, and ought to be well considered and weighed, before ventured on. Still, if concluded on, a determined will and mature calculation should accompany the undertaking, which is to cast a *life-long* destiny—no flinching, for on manly resolution depends success. It would always be better if those persons desiring to emigrate to Texas, with their families, could come and look at the country, before a final remove; but distance, expense, and consumption of time, generally prevent such cautionary measures. Therefore, a knowledge of the country must be acquired through the perceptions and judgments of other people; and, as men are governed in their views and representations by many causes, emigrants are frequently unhappily disappointed, and more especially if they are from the older States: the discomforts of a log-cabin; the jolting of an ox-cart, which takes the place here of a pleasure carriage; the homely roughness of the neighbors; illy suit the tastes of fastidious persons. But hardships, privations, and discomforts, must ever, for a season, be endured by the emigrant.

The sparseness and distance of neighbors (and perhaps the nearest may be a Dutchman), makes it lonely for the family at first, but this dreariness soon wears off; the scenery is new, everything around is strange and unusual; the prairies, the herbage, the trees and rocks belong, as it were, to a different creation; even the sky above is not the native heaven, the phenomena of Nature seem to be governed by new and strange laws.

The contemplation of these fills up the dreary void left in the mind by far distant objects, and the affections of the family gradually become concentrated on the new home. A few years of quiet industry pass by, the neighborhood fills up apace, small villages start up and grow with unprecedented rapidity, roads and cross roads and parallel roads mark the country, stores and churches and schools are not distant in any direction, markets and speculators come in competition for the coveted productions of the soil, people of wealth and extended enterprise begin to settle about, and lands and property rise higher and higher, until the emigrant finds himself wealthy, his family are able to have the comforts and luxuries of refined society, and to educate and bring up their children in the ways of respectability and usefulness.

Emigrants should bring with them as many garden and other rare seeds as convenient; the more common seeds will be found in the country. Everything else let them turn into money, for it will be more expensive to bring cumbrous household and farming implements than to purchase them, unless they intend settling near the coast.

Emigrants from the Eastern, Southern-Atlantic, and Middle States, will do best to come by sea to Galveston, or Matagorda Bay.

The most economical, profitable, and pleasant way for settling in a new country, is to proceed after this plan: — Where there are eight or ten families in a neighborhood, who have made up their minds to seek a new home, let them organize themselves into a company, under written articles of agreement; each head of a family binds himself to furnish so much money for the general object; then ascertain the wholesale cost of transporting all of the families and effects to the shores of Texas; one of the members, a shrewd, capable man, is sent out to bargain for a suitable tract of land, that, when divided, shall suit all of their several wants; the first year they farm in common, and until, by their united labor, each family is furnished with a dwelling, fences, &c.; after that, when a good supply of grain has been raised to furnish the community until the next harvest, the land can be divided among them according to their respective advancements of capital. In this way a thrifty settlement at once arises, and becomes the nucleus around which other emigrants are constantly attracted, and in this manner can be purchased much cheaper. The dreariness of a solitary emigrant's life is never felt by members of a community, and the comforts and advantages of homogeneous society are retained, while land and property become immediately enhanced two or three hundred per cent.

Western Texas is an extensive country, and has many varieties of soil and productions. Excepting on the bottom lands of the rivers and water-courses, the people are mostly engaged in stock-raising; many of them exclusively, and others in connection with farming. This region, below 30°, and west to the Rio Grande, is very subject to long droughts during the summer; still the crops on the bottom lands seldom fail. No portion is sickly, but all is favorable to the life and energy of man and beast. The principal grass on the prairies is the far-famed *mesquit*, deservedly renowned for its universal abundance and nutritious qualities; during all the winter season, and after it has become sere and yellow, cattle and horses will eat it with the same avidity and benefit as when green. Of late years, large quantities have been cured and baled for distant markets, and the U. S. military posts always prefer it for their cavalry horses to the imported hay from cultivated grasses.

I would advise emigrants who want good and cheap lands, with plenty of mesquit prairie for stock range, to purchase on the Nueces, Rio Frio, or some of their branches. This is a desirable part of Western Texas, and has as many natural advantages as can be asked by any reasonable man. Land sells at from $1·50 to $2·00 per acre. The timber on the streams is *peccan*, *hackberry*, several kinds of *oak*, *cypress*, and *mulberry ;* on the prairies are much *live oak* and *mesquit* timber.

There are many other portions of the west where the land is better adapted for raising cotton, but none that will so well suit the emigrant of moderate capital, and fill the measure of his utmost expectations and desires.

CHAPTER II.

DESCRIPTION OF COUNTIES.

ANDERSON COUNTY.

THIS is an interior county, on the Trinity River, the centre being 180 miles from Galveston. The Trinity is navigable for steamers far above this county, though not at all times to be depended on. The face of the country is level, with timber lands on the streams, and luxuriant prairies between. Palestine, the county-seat, is well situated in the centre of this flourishing county. There is very little rock, and the soil is easily cultivated. Palestine contains a population of 1200. The business of the town is confined to retail trade with the surrounding country; there are twelve stores here, among which are two drug stores and a book store; all seem to be prospering. The county gives one thousand votes, and makes about 300,000 lbs. cotton.

The land is quite fertile, producing, on an average, one bale, or 500 lbs. clean cotton per acre, or thirty bushels of corn to the acre. Cotton seems to be the best adapted to the lands of this county, but wheat grows and produces well. The crops are sent down the Trinity to Galveston, or hauled to Houston by ox teams.

BURLESON COUNTY.

This county lies north, and adjoining Washington County, and has been settled for many years; the lands are fertile; distance of county-seat from Galveston is 150 miles, and from Matagorda 150 miles. Though the crops of 1856 were short in this rich county, the farmers made a large amount of bacon, depending altogether on the oak mast; farmers from other counties during the last fall drove many hogs here to fatten; still there was an abundance of swine food for all. The lands of Burleson County are steadily advancing in value. Unimproved bottom lands are worth $10 per acre; uplands are worth from two to three dollars per acre.

The "Old San Antonio road," which divides Robertson and Brazos counties, east of the Brazos River, passes centrally through Burleson County from east to west. This county is also largely interested in stock-raising, and it is said that there are now at least $50,000 worth of beeves ready for market.

Caldwell, the county-seat, is a pleasant, healthy, and flourishing village, situated on the San Antonio road, about eleven miles west of the Brazos; it contains seven dry goods and other stores, and fortunately but one place where liquor is sold. There are good male and female schools, affording excellent opportunities of educating children. A Masonic Lodge, a Temple of Honor, and one of the most capacious and best built brick court-houses in the State; also a Methodist and a Baptist church building. The population numbers about 300, who are moral in their habits, intelligent, and courteous to strangers.

CORYELL COUNTY.

This county takes its name from a creek, which derived its name from a man named Coryell, who had a survey of land on this creek, and was killed several years ago by Indians. The county is divided into prairie, timber, mountains and valleys. The Leon River is the main stream, which runs into the county about ten miles south of the north-west corner; it then makes a bend more southward, and runs near the centre of the county; thence out to the south of the north-east corner, about eight miles. The main tributary of the Leon, on the north, is Coryell creek, which has its source near the north-west corner of the county, and runs south-east to the Leon, about twelve miles below Gatesville. East of this stream and the Leon is prairie, good soil, and fine stock range. The prairies will soon be dotted over with settlements and small farms, for this is a paradise for the small farmer. Rails delivered on this prairie cost from $2·50 to $3 per hundred. There are mountains on both sides of Coryell creek, which furnish large quantities of cedar. The valleys on this creek are small; the Leon has much valley land, which produces grain of all kinds in abundance. There is also some sandy post oak land, excellent for hog-raising, from the abundance of mast.

There are several small streams running into the Leon from the south-west side, the largest of which are Plum creek, Henson's creek, and Owl creek; the first of these empties into the Leon above Gatesville, the second ten miles below, and the third below the county line, in Bell County.

These streams have all their hills and valleys. Many beautiful situations for small farms are to be found in the valleys, with first-rate soil, and timber on the hills and creeks. Hogs, sheep, goats, and small stocks of neat cattle do well, and afford an easy income to the farmer, with very little trouble and outlay. Cowhouse creek is a large, clear stream, having its source in Comanche County, and runs east through this county; its valleys of good land are from a quarter of a mile to two miles wide, chiefly prairie, with timber on the creeks for building, fire-wood, and fencing; a very good stock country, and well watered. This stream empties into the Leon in Bell County, six miles above Belton. Fencing, on Cowhouse creek, costs about $2 per hundred rails. There has been no cotton planted in this county; wheat is a staple crop. There are but two mills in the county; one owned by R. G. Grant, a quarter of a mile from Gatesville, on the Leon; the other belonging to Mr. Jones, near the Bell County line, on the same stream. This year, as is very well known, was so very dry that it is no criterion; in common seasons, mills on the Leon will run nine months in the year. All of the streams have good mill-seats, yet unoccupied.

Gatesville, the county-seat, is the only town. It is pleasantly situated on the north side of the Leon, on an eminence. The town consists of about thirty houses, including court-house, jail, shops, and offices. There are three stores, two hotels, three lawyers, two physicians, and several mechanics; the professional men have very little business. The population is from all the States, but principally from the western portion of the Southern States. Society is good, and churches and school-houses are being built in various parts of the county. Improved lands can be bought at from $3 to $6 per acre; unimproved lands at from $1·50 to $4 per acre. There are yet some choice tracts of vacant land in this county. From Austin to Gatesville is 80 miles; the nearest and best route being by Georgetown, thence by the Fort Gates military road.

DENTON COUNTY.

This is a new county, in the extreme northern part of the State. It is a good grain and fruit region; surface level and easy to cultivate, being divided into prairie and timber; frequently large crops of wheat and corn have been planted, with only the assistance of one horse and a plough, to break the soil.

Denton is the name of the county-seat, which is situate six miles west of Alton, the former county-town; it is a delightful place, located in a neck of prairie, connecting with the Grand Prairie. There are 600 voters in this county, and immigration is rolling in like a flood-tide in a northern latitude. Pork is worth 2½ cents per lb.; flour $3·50 per cwt.; corn 60 to 70 cents per bushel; and wheat 75 cents. The present low price and abundance of provisions offer great facilities to the emigrant, and those persons who desire new homes cannot do better in any part of the United States than in Denton. This county has good cattle and hog ranges; being situated in the "Cross Timber" country, there is a superabundance of mast, and hogs fatten on it, without an ear of corn. Distance from the town of Alton to Austin is 200 miles.

ELLIS COUNTY.

This county is in the northern part of the State, and above the Pacific Railroad.

Waxahatchie, the county-seat, is decidedly a beautiful and rising town, situated contiguous to a good supply of timber, blessed with plenty of excellent water, healthful, and surrounded with the best wheat-growing region to be found. Emigrants with small means, and who desire to cultivate a remunerating soil, cannot do better than go to Ellis County. Sheep, cattle, and horses do well, and have an abundance of free pasture.

GOLIAD COUNTY.

This is a western county, and lies near the Gulf of Mexico; the San Antonio River runs through the centre; there are several smaller streams. The land is good for cotton and corn, that on the Blanco and Medio being very superior. For stock-raising this region has not its equal out of Texas. Lands are worth from $1·50 to $3 per acre; immigration is now turning in this direction, and lands will rise in price. The climate is healthful at all seasons, it being sufficiently near the Gulf to enjoy the exhilarating breezes in summer and modifying influences in winter. Stranger, if you have a small money capital, and are blessed with a large family, go to Goliad County while yet the lands are cheap, acquire a few hundred acres, buy a few cattle and horses, and the foundation of your fortune is laid, firmly and securely; you never will regret the move if you take this advice; your only sorrow will be that you did not come sooner.

This charming county lies about thirty miles north of Aransas Bay, and is well situated for the cultivation of cotton, and stock-raising. It has an intelligent and refined population, and is favored with two well-conducted literary institutions: Aranama College and Paine Female Institute. The town of Goliad is the county-seat; the old Mexican town of La Bahia is situated opposite Goliad. The view from the heights of La Bahia is indeed an enchanting one, and seems especially so when bathed in the sunlight of a serene and cloudless sky. On the left, as you ascend to the mission, rise romantic hills, sloping into various plains, which are, even in winter, covered with merry green, and through which the rippling surface of the meandering San Antonio flows, in all its sparkling and peculiar beauty. The lovely town of Goliad, with its neat white houses, amidst overshadowing trees, lies beyond; and towering above them all, upon opposite summits, stand Aranama College and Paine Female Institute. On the right of the ascent an almost interminable, but undulating prairie, stretches far around, presenting a scene of classic and picturesque beauty. The old mission church is still in a state of preservation, though surrounded by broken walls and crumbling bastions; the hand of modern renovation has in a measure rendered the interior fit for religious worship.

GONZALES COUNTY.

This county is west of the Colorado, and was settled in the early history of Texas. There are extensive deposits of iron and coal in this county. The distance from Gonzales to Port Lavacca is 75 miles. The lands of this county are fertile and easily cultivated. A recent writer says of the land on Peach Creek, in that county: — "It is as fertile as the river valleys, and has the immense advantage of sustaining drought with less injury to the crops; last year (1856), notwithstanding the unprecedented drought, the yield of corn averaged from twenty to forty bushels. The scenery is beautiful, of the description known as rolling prairies. The long slopes are covered with thick, soft grass, and crowned with groves of noble live oaks and other trees; building-stone is found in abundance throughout the county, and the numerous little brooks of clear running water afford every advantage for stock. Sheep are raised in considerable numbers, and are healthy and very profitable. Hogs, likewise, are abundant and thrifty, and increase rapidly.

This desirable region is rapidly filling up with intelligent and substantial men; people of means, liberality, and enterprise, who will take much interest in building up churches and schools, to meet the increasing necessities of the country. It will be well for emigrants with capital to take a look at this county.

HAYS COUNTY.

This is a western county; the surface is diversified by hill, valley, rivulet, and brook. It is a good stock-raising and farming county, and has a genial climate; here are some of the most valuable water privileges in the State of Texas; coal, iron, salt, and other minerals and metals, are said to abound. The distance from the centre of the county to Port Lavacca is 135 miles. San Marcos is a town at the Springs of that name, and Stringtown is a settlement built along a beautiful valley at the foot of the mountain range; these are both charming sites. A recent writer says: — "There is not a more beautiful and romantic spot than the San Marcos country; on the north the mountains afford protection against the 'Northers,' on the south the country spreads out in beautiful prairie valleys, which make most excellent farms; on many of them are now (January, 1857) large fields of wheat in a flourishing condition, which cover the earth with a lovely mantle of deep green." San Marcos contains several stores, a tavern, church, and several other public buildings; it is situated on the west side of the San Marcos River, a beautiful, transparent stream, which gushes out in a large spring, forming a miniature Switzer lake at the foot of a mountain. This stream constitutes a splendid water-power, capable of moving any amount of machinery; a cotton factory is under progress at this place; a large manufacturing town will arise here, equal in importance and wealth to any of the New England towns. The San Antonio and Gulf Railroad, now in vigorous progress of construction, with every guarantee of speedy completion, will give to this western portion of the State an impetus on the road to prosperity and aggrandizement which cannot now be realized. Lands can now be bought in this county at from $2 to $10 per acre.

HENDERSON, AND ADJOINING COUNTIES.

This is the next county above Anderson, on the Trinity River, and is fast filling up with an industrious population. Public attention has been more turned to this section of late, and we are convinced, from the inducements offered, that no portion of Texas will improve, for the next ten years, in increased population and wealth, more than it will. As an average of the production of the timbered counties, we would say that, in cotton, through a series of years, the farmers would raise 800 pounds per acre; a No. 1 farmer could safely calculate on 1000 or 1200 pounds. Farmers do not generally take so much pains in the cultivation of their lands as in most of the other Southern States; they seem to get indolent and careless, which is partly caused by the fact, that here a man can raise more with a little labor than is usual elsewhere. The lands of this county are well adapted to corn; even in the driest years they will produce from twenty-five to thirty bushels per acre; they also produce good wheat where it has been tried, very little having been planted until within the last two years. Last fall (1857) more was planted than usual, and it is now very promising. We are satisfied that this is one of the healthiest regions under the sun; here there are but few local causes for disease; and the water is pure and wholesome. Lands are cheap in this portion of Texas; in Rusk, Cherokee, Smith, Anderson, and Harrison counties, which are in the highest state of improvement of any in the State, and the most densely populated, they are worth from $2·50 to $10 per acre. It is beyond question a very superior hog country; most of the farmers feed their hogs but little, they becoming sufficiently fat to kill by running in the woods; meat this season has averaged about 4½ cents net; corn is worth 50 cents per bushel; cattle about $6 per head by the stock; poultry abundant; butter 20 cents per pound. The lands lay generally level, and there are very few rocks to interfere with cultivation. There are, from Henderson to Tyler, in Smith County, numerous little towns springing up, in all of which the school-house and church are prominent establishments. The town of Tyler is a considerable place, beautifully laid off, and is the county-seat of Smith County. The court-house is a fine sightly brick building; the houses are all good; some of the dwelling-houses are models of elegance and comfort. Education is in a flourishing condition, and measures are on foot to build a University at Tyler.

Kickapoo, in Anderson county, is described as a thriving town, and doing considerable business.

The lands in this section are red, sandy, and very productive: there is much timber and little prairie. Corn was plenty last fall, and sold for fifty cents per bushel. There is not much stock in this region, but it is well adapted to swine, and pork is very cheap every fall.

Sumpter, in Trinity county, is a new place, it being only two years old; but gives evidence of much public spirit and enterprise.

A court-house has been commenced, at this place: the material is of brick, and the building is to be two stories high, and of ample dimensions.

JOHNSON COUNTY.

This county lies above the line of the Pacific railroad (32°), and is in the midst of the wheat region. It is of quite recent organization: the lands are good and very cheap; the prairies are said to be of the best quality. We learn that the population is increasing, by large and substantial additions of emigrants. The famous heights, "Pilot Knob" and "Camanche Peak," are in this county. Distance from Matagorda to the centre is 250 miles, and from Port Lavacca is 250 miles.

KERR COUNTY.

This is a new county, in the western portion of the State. The country is much broken, and diversified with hills and valleys: the hillside springs send forth their brooks and rills, to make this charming region more lovely, and permeate the virgin soil with their life-giving powers. Stock of all kinds do well; and it is said that the soil and climate are well adapted to the extensive culture of grapes and other fruit.

This county is fast filling up with substantial settlers, who are reaping the benefits of cheap lands. It is one of the most healthful counties in the State. There are many indications of valuable metals and minerals here.

Distance from the centre of the county to Port Lavacca, is 180 miles.

CHAPTER III.

DESCRIPTION OF COUNTIES (CONTINUED).

MEDINA COUNTY.

A great deal of the surface of this county is made up of hill, dale, valley, and prairie: it is well watered with mountain streamlets, on some of which thriving manufacturing villages will arise. This is a western county, and is settled mostly with foreigners. Castroville, the seat of Medina county, is most happily located, with regard to fertility of soil, abundance of water, timber and grazing lands. It extends over a level prairie, following the meanderings of the Medina; is surrounded by gentle, well-timbered hills, from the top of which the eye embraces the whole valley, which has been made a perfect garden by the settlers. Twelve years ago, Castroville was one of the most attractive hunting-grounds of the fierce Lipan Indians. It derives its name from Mr. Castro, who obtained, in 1842, a contract from the Texan government to introduce foreign emigrants. The majority of the settlers are from the French and German borders of the Rhine, and seem to be hardy and industrious citizens. They speak German

4

amongst themselves, although most of them have sufficient knowledge of the English language to be able to transact business with Americans. There are three schools in this thriving place, one of which is free; and the rising generation are receiving inestimable advantages. I do really believe that the foreign children acquire an education, in English, sooner than those born of American parents. I have frequently seen German children, of ten or twelve years old, who were much further advanced than their compeers of more favored birth.

The town numbers 1000 souls, within the incorporated limits, independent of a large rural population in the close vicinity.

The court-house is a substantial building: there is also a Catholic and a Protestant church, the former of which is an elegant stone building, and would be creditable to a wealthier community. Three large stores, several smaller ones, a brewery, and an excellent water-power grist-mill, all doing good business, indicate thrift and prosperity. The dwellings and improvements show that the inhabitants have exchanged their dejected condition, in their *faderland*, for comfort and abundance.

The principal wealth of this county arises from corn-planting, and raising cattle, horses, hogs, and poultry; for which a ready market is found in the military posts farther west. The hauling of stores and subsistence for the army is also an important and profitable branch of business.

Three settlements, viz., Quihi, Vandenburgh, and Dhanis, are west of Castroville, and improve fast. This portion of Texas will, in a few years, be thickly settled; and American enterprise and energy, joined with German industry, perseverance, and frugality, will make it the wealthiest portion of our State.

MATAGORDA COUNTY.

This county is bounded on the north by Wharton county, on the south by the Gulf of Mexico, on the east by Brazoria county and Gulf of Mexico, and on the west by Calhoun and Jackson counties.

The area is 1334 square miles, about 510 of which are covered by Matagorda and Trespalacios bays. The general surface is level, and classed as bottom and prairie lands. There is much alluvial bottom-land in this county, which is nearly all well adapted to the culture of cotton, sugar-cane, rice, and Indian corn, besides many other productions of minor importance —sugar and cotton being, at present, the staples for exportation.

The alluvial soils, or what is called *the* planting lands, lie on the east side of the Colorado river, and are the bottom-lands, or deposits, which it has taken untold ages to accumulate on Old Caney, Peach Creek, Sinville Bayou, and Live Oak. There are several other smaller streams on the east side of the Colorado, with good bottom-lands and timber, not extensive enough for plantations, but well adapted for small farms and stock-raisers.

The Colorado lands, in the lower part of the county, are subject to occasional overflows, with the exception of some choice spots; and, therefore, notwithstanding the fertility of the soil, not so desirable. Old Caney, the most important stream, in an agricultural point of view, runs S. E. and N. W. through the county, and its dry bed opens into the Colorado in Wharton county: from the immense alluvial bottoms on each side, its present diminished waters, and deep bed, it is supposed to have been the former main channel of the Colorado. It is several miles below the intersection with the Colorado, before Caney contains any water: its banks never overflow from heavy rains, and it is very little else, above tide-water, than a large prairie drain: it runs into the Gulf of Mexico, in the south-eastern part of the county: it is also connected with the head of Matagorda bay by a large canal, half a mile long, which is navigable for the largest lighters. The Caney alluvial deposit is, in many places, thirty feet deep; and its surface is covered with forests of gigantic oaks, elms, red cedar, and cane and wild-peach brakes. The cane and peach lands are considered best for cultivation, and have been so nicely compounded and proportioned in the laboratory of Nature, that no other soils in the world are equal, for the production of cotton, sugar-cane, and corn. The Bay of Matagorda, a large body of water, almost wholly within this county, is separated from the Gulf of Mexico, and formed by the "Matagorda

Peninsula," a strip of land sixty-five miles long, and averaging one mile wide. It lies nearly N. E. and S. W., and is inhabited by small farmers and stock-raisers. A portion of this land, lying back from the Gulf, is an excellent, dark, sandy soil, easily cultivated, and very productive in all kinds of vegetation which is not injured by the sea-breeze. Notwithstanding high winds, a crop of sugar-cane was raised here, several years since, and manufactured into first quality sugar, on the premises. There is no healthier region in the world than Matagorda Peninsula; and many invalids have been restored to sound health through the happy influences of its pure air and sea-bathing. Game and fish can be obtained here, at all seasons, with ease and in abundance; and I dare assert, that I have never seen a place where poor men, by agricultural pursuits, may live so easily, and so soon become independent.

The bays of this county are, Matagorda, Trespalacios, and a portion of Karanqua. The timber is live-oak, post-oak, pin-oak, pecan, ash, cotton-wood, white and red elm, mulberry, red-cedar, and several other kinds, of minor importance.

We have no rock or stone, excepting conglomerates; no minerals excepting salt. In the sea-board part of the county, at from five to ten feet below the surface, is found an abundance of strongly impregnated salt water, of much greater density than sea water. The manufacture of salt used to be carried on, in this county, during the days of "Austin's

Colonial Government," to a considerable extent; but scarcity of fuel caused its abandonment: it is thought, however, that solar evaporation may be profitably employed. The water-courses in this county are, the Trespalacios and Colorado rivers, Peyton's Creek, Caney, Peach Creek, Linville Bayou, and Live Oak Creek, all of which are unimportant for navigation, excepting the Colorado, Trespalacios, and Caney: the former is one of the most important rivers in the State, and will, with some little outlay for clearing out obstructions of fallen timber, become navigable for steamers to Austin, about 300 miles by road. An appropriation of $50,000 was made, by our last legislature, for this object; which sum, if properly expended, will bring the people of the Colorado valley in easy communication with Matagorda bay. This river is the great natural high-road for the bulky, but valuable, productions of all that region; and Matagorda bay is the natural terminus of the road, in Texas. At some point on the bay will be established the receptacle for the masses of raw products, as they are floated down the stream for a distant mart; and here, in transit, will arrive, in exchange, the "purples and fine linens" of luxury and extravagance, together with the more useful articles of husbandry, arts, and manufactures — all of which, by means of the interior thoroughfare, will be quickly diffused throughout all the regions round about. The various and vast amount of productions from the interior will attract to our bay the shipping and wealth of distant States, and build up, at some favored spot, a city of no inconsiderable size. It is no enigma where that sea-port town will be; for Nature has favored Palacios, above all other sites, with the advantages of a great seaport town. It is estimated that the cotton crop of 1857, in the five counties below Travis, through which the Colorado runs, will produce at least 60,000 bales; not to reckon the amount produced in the adjoining tributary counties, and the other productions which seek a market. All this now goes through the slow, expensive, and destructive process of being hauled to Houston, or some other inconvenient place. Trespalacios and Caney are navigable, for large lighters and small steamers, a short distance above tide-water.

This county, like all of the seaboard country, is too level for much regular propelling water power; however, there is a short stream called Mill Creek, running past "Selkirk's Islands" from the west branch of the Colorado to the east, which has a steady fall of three or four feet, and could be used for machinery.

The grazing facilities are equal in this county to any in the State, owing to the abundance of fresh water, the fertility of the prairie soil, and the peculiarly mild winters; the sea atmosphere mollifies the rigors of January and February, and renders pleasant the summer months.

The kinds of animals kept by those persons who make a business of stock-raising, are horses and neat cattle, excepting on the "Peninsula," where several flocks of sheep are kept; these latter animals thrive nowhere else on the seaboard.

West of the Colorado, and all that portion of Matagorda County watered by the "Trespalacios," is exclusively occupied by stock-raisers and small farmers, to both of which lucrative callings the Trespalacios lands, and those bordering on the Colorado, are well adapted; $300 or $400 invested here in cattle, breed-horses, and land, render an industrious man independent in a few years. Land here can be purchased at from $1 to $2 per acre, stock cattle at $5 per head, and brood-mares for $25 each. Planters would scorn to look at this poor region, as the lands of "Old Caney" are too rich and productive for them to be content with any but the best soil in the world; but to be a planter requires more capital than belongs to a poor man, and none but a planter should think of the alluvial bottoms.

The towns in this county are Matagorda and Palacios; the former is a very old place, and had at one time a considerable commerce with foreign countries, and trade with the interior and Mexico; in fact, during the revolutionary period, it was a frontier town. It is situated on Matagorda Bay, which lies in front and to the south, and the east branch of the Colorado forms the corporate limits on the northwest, and disembogues into the bay about one mile below the town.

All shipping drawing over seven feet water are obliged to come to anchor eight miles below.

The town contains about 1200 inhabitants, who rank high in the social scale, on the score of morality, hospitality, and superior intellectual endowments; they are also very fashionable in their attire and habits, and in religion are generally Episcopalians. There are many fine buildings, and several commodious public edifices. The latter is little more, at present, than a town site, or paper town; nevertheless, it is the most important place in Texas, considered in a commercial point of view. Palacios was surveyed and laid off several years since, west of the Colorado River, on a high point of land between Matagorda and Trespalacios bays, and is in a more favorable position for a large seaport town than any other on the whole coast of Texas; the water in front of the town, within sixty yards, being eleven feet deep, with safe anchorage, and good holding ground, and is perfectly protected from all prevailing winds; in fact, the harbor is so secure, that small boats, in passing up and down the bay, always seek refuge here in rough or threatening weather. The distance to the Pass, or entrance from the Gulf of Mexico, is twenty miles south by west, with good and open seaway. The largest class steamers and sail vessels that enter the bay can come directly up to Palacios, with all sails set, or steam up, without impediment or risk of danger. This place being firmly seated on the mainland, is not so subject to serious damage from the destructive hurricanes, or *cyclones*, which visit our coast now and then, as are other places more exposed, and on lower and more insecure locations; in fact, within the last two or three years, people have began to think that the islands and peninsulas along the Texas and Louisiana coast are unsafe for human abiding places; and to any one who experienced our memorable storm of September 18th, 1854, or beheld the sad relics of the "Last Island" disaster, the *debris* lands of the Gulf coast will hardly appear suitable and pleasant for *permanent* settlements. And Galveston Island, with all its boasted accumulation of people, habitations, wealth, trade, and commerce, is but a waif of the ocean, a locality but of yesterday, a resting-place for drift and sea-birds, liable, at any moment, and certain, at no distant day, of being engulfed and submerged by the self-same power that gave it form. Neither is it possible for all the skilful devices of mortal man to protect this *doomed* place against the impending danger; the terrible power of a hurricane cannot be calculated, much less resisted; its strength is the awful power of combined elements, and the waters of the mighty deep are made a fearful and sudden engine of destruction; a part of the ocean itself, as it were, is lifted up and onward, and goes rolling, hurling, and crashing over the low coast, with all the conceivable fury and end of matter attributable to the final day, carrying devastation, death, and destruction to all created beings, obliterating the works of man, and frequently blotting out the low islands and coast altogether. I should as soon think of founding a city on an iceberg as on Galveston Island, if I looked to its safety and perpetuity.

Palacios, from its water facilities, and otherwise favorable locality, seems to have been pre-eminently designed by Nature for the emporium seaport town of Texas, and, as soon as trade and commerce shall have been turned to their proper channels, will take such position.

LLANO COUNTY.

This is a new county, in Western Texas, and in that region where much land was granted to the German colonists: the Colorado river forms its eastern boundary, and the Rio Llano runs through the county. A writer in the Texas Christian Advocate says: "Twenty miles from the mouth of the latter river is the county-seat. It is, like all other Western streams, clear and swift. Five miles below the mouth is the Sandy, a small stream. There are many indications of the precious metals in this section. The soil is not of great depth, and is underlaid with immense strata of rock, embracing granitic, sandstone, and thirteen varieties of quartz rock. As a stock and fruit country, it is unsurpassed. The Pack-saddle mountain may be seen from twenty to fifty miles, and is separated, by a valley of two miles wide, from all other hills or mountains: it has two abrupt ascents, called domes, which give to the mountain much of its grandeur. Honey Creek Cove lies within three miles of the Pack-saddle, and is inhabited by a number of settlers. The creek empties into the Llano, and has a number of falls, some as high as sixty feet; and there is much water-power, and situations well adapted to machinery. The whole valley, or cove, can be irrigated at a small expense; and will, I have no doubt, at no distant day, be converted into a vineyard."

NAVARRO COUNTY.

The Pacific railroad line runs through the centre of this county. Its organization is of recent date, but it has already become quite populous. This is a prairie country, with timber on the streams: soil is excellent for all the grains, and more especially for wheat. It is said that three times as much wheat is sown this year (1857) as last. Corn is worth seventy-five cents per bushel; the wants of recent emigrants keeping up the price much above the cost of production. Pork usually sells for about four cents per pound. The expense of getting goods from Houston is 12½ cents per pound.

An abundance of good and low-priced land can be bought in Navarro; and emigrants will find a cordial welcome, abundance of supplies, and a healthful climate, and, what is quite as important, good society.

Distance from Houston to centre of county is 175 miles, from Galveston 200 miles, and from Matagorda 250 miles.

The lands of this county are universally fertile, and easy of cultivation, the water good, and stock range excellent. Corn, beef, and pork are, at this date (Feb. 1857), abundant and cheap; and there will be no lack for the incoming emigration of this year. There are three steam-mills in operation, sawing lumber, and grinding wheat and corn. The flour of this and the adjoining counties is superior to any that we get from abroad. Corsicana is the county-seat, and a place of considerable importance: there is a Presbyterian church, a female school edifice, a Masonic and an Odd-Fellows' lodge, two taverns, two drug-stores, *ten lawyers*, and half-a-dozen doctors, more or less. The town of Dresden is fourteen miles west of Corsicana, in a densely populated neighborhood, and surrounded by rich lands. Taos is situated on the Trinity river, eighteen miles from Corsicana, and lies at the crossing of the Pacific railroad.

Navarro is one of the most thriving counties of the State; and was, but a few years since, an untraversed wilderness.

ORANGE COUNTY.

This county is at the head of Sabine Lake, and is separated from Louisiana by the Sabine river: it is a well-timbered county, having very little prairie. All of the coast towns in Texas receive from this region their finest cypress lumber.

The bend in the Sabine, at the town of Madison, is like the Mississippi at New Orleans, on a small scale, and Madison is a miniature New Orleans. The

5

houses are tastefully built, and the place has the appearance of quite a city: the principal business done here is the lumber trade. A number of steam saw-mills are erected in and around the place, and the whole Sabine swamp abounding with the finest cypress in the world, lumber is both cheap and abundant. Immense quantities of shingles are also manufactured, and sell at about $2·50 per thousand. This town is on the west bank of the Sabine, about thirty-five miles from the sea-coast, or Sabine Pass, a small town on the Gulf of Mexico. About twenty-five miles of this distance is through a beautiful lake, having an average depth of seven feet, and free from shoals. Sabine Lake is surrounded with low prairie land, which makes a fine stock range. On the way from Sabine Pass, Jefferson county, to Madison, Orange county, the traveller first crosses this lake; this brings him to the mouth of the beautiful Sabine; twelve miles up the Sabine brings him to Madison. This distance the river runs through a low, marshy country; but the navigation to Madison cannot be excelled by any river in the United States. Just above Madison, the timber begins; and then, for 600 miles, the Sabine runs through a cypress swamp, and this world of timber must be manufactured to supply the western coast of Texas. There is, also, plenty of yellow pine, white oak, and timber of other kinds, necessary for ship building.

PARKER COUNTY.

This is a newly organized and settled county, on the Upper Brazos, and above the line of the Pacific railroad. A desirable region for small farmers—which meed of praise is alike due to all of the adjoining counties.

Weatherford, a new town, and the county-seat, is rapidly increasing. Not twelve months ago, the site was laid out: there are already a court-house, and several other public buildings, one hotel, several stores, private dwelling-houses, and other marks of civilization. The town is pleasantly situated, in the "Upper Cross Timbers," and is well supplied with good water, and with an abundance of timber. There is a fine chalybeate spring about one-fourth of a mile from the public square: it is said to possess valuable medical properties.

Distance from Matagorda 240 miles.

POLK COUNTY.

This county lies on both sides of the Trinity river, and is steadily increasing in population. The many streams flowing into the Trinity, as well as the East Fork of San Jacinto, the Big Sandy, and the Trinity itself, have large bodies of rich land, suitable for the cotton-planters; and here is the "Big Thicket," celebrated over the whole State for its extraordinarily fertile soil. The rich prairies of this county afford free commons to any number of herdsmen.

Livingston, the county-seat, is a small but thriving

town, substantially and tastefully built. Distance from Livingston to Galveston is ninety miles. Moscow, another town in this county, is a considerable place, and fast increasing. The Henderson and Gulf railroad, when completed, will make this county to blossom as the Garden of Eden.

ROBERTSON COUNTY.

The 31st parallel of latitude runs through the centre of this county, and, being situated very nearly in the centre of the settled portion of the State, equidistant from the Gulf of Mexico on the south, the grain region on the north, the Sabine on the east, and the Rio Grande on the west, many advantages are combined that are rarely to be found in any other section of our State. This county is bounded on its entire west, for over thirty miles, by the Brazos River, and on the east by the Navasoto. It is calculated that the Brazos valley, so far as it bounds this county, will average four miles wide, and in point of fertility of soil is unsurpassed by any lands, not only in Texas, but in the world. The face of the upland country, as the traveller leaves the Brazos valley, is exceedingly beautiful and desirable. The ascent to the divide between the two rivers (the Navasoto and Brazos), is an almost imperceptible rise through a succession of beautiful sweeps, or long slopes of country, gradual in rise and declivity, till you reach the ridge that separates their waters. The uplands each way, or to either stream, are heavily set with fine post oak timber, and are of a deep mulatto or yellow cast, interspersed with creeks running through at convenient intervals, affording good bottom lands and plenty of stock-water in the driest season.

The lands of this county are well adapted to the production of the finest cotton raised in the cotton-growing States.

Unimproved lands are now worth $1·50 to $3·50; these lands, in a year or two, will be worth three or four times as much.

The new county-seat of Robertson County is Owensville, situated sixteen miles north of Wheelock, on a beautiful, elevated spot of ground, pretty nearly in the centre of the county, and on the dividing ridge between the Brazos and Navasoto, and within one mile and a half of the proposed route for the Houston, Red River, and Central Texas Railroad. A fine court-house, a jail, and female academy, have already been erected. Emigrants will do well to turn their attention in this direction.

RUSK COUNTY.

This is an interior eastern county, crossing the line of the Pacific railroad: the soil is good, and produces all the grains: much cotton is also raised in this county.

Henderson is the principal town, or city; for it is a place of much size and note, having many fine brick buildings, school-houses, churches, and other public edifices.

Rusk county, at last general election, gave 2000 votes. Distance from Galveston to Henderson is 175 miles.

SMITH COUNTY.

This county lies above the 32d degree of north latitude, and in the north-eastern part of the State; it is a well-watered county, and has plenty of timber; the soil is fertile and productive, and climate healthy. Tyler, the county-seat, is directly on the line of the Pacific Railroad; it is already a place of considerable importance, and contains many buildings of taste and beauty. The public square is very large, and in the centre is a natural mound, on which the court-house is built. Education has received the especial attention of the people of Tyler, as is evidenced by the commodious buildings devoted to learning.

TRAVIS COUNTY.

This county lies on both sides of the Colorado River, about 150 miles from its mouth. Austin, the seat of the State Government, is in this county, on the east side of the Colorado River.

This is a good farming and stock-raising county, and is fast increasing in population and wealth; there is plenty of timber for building and fencing, and a superior kind of stone, with which the public edifices and many private residences have been erected.

The total amount of taxation of this county is $6,262·98. There are 2399 negroes, 4326 horses, and

16,928 head of neat cattle, besides a large number of hogs, and some flocks of sheep.

Lands near Austin are held at high prices, but at some distance from town can be bought at moderate rates. When the slight obstructions in the Colorado have been cleared out, steam navigation will be open from Matagorda Bay to the city of Austin, for several months in the year.

VAN ZANDT COUNTY.

This is a new county, above the line of the Pacific Railroad reserve, containing nearly all good land, and is well watered; the face of the country is level, with timber on the streams, and small prairies between. The land is easy to cultivate, and produces sure and abundant crops of wheat and Indian corn. The climate is healthy. Land can now be bought for $1 per acre, which would be worth $50 per acre if there were facilities for getting produce to the coast. The Henderson and Galveston Railroad, now in progress of construction, will develop this beautiful region of county. Distance from Canton, the county-seat, to Galveston, 200 miles.

WASHINGTON COUNTY.

Washington County is on the west side of the Brazos, that river marking the eastern boundary. This county was settled in the early history of Texas, and still numbers among its inhabitants many of the pioneer families, who are now enjoying, in comfortable independence, their hard-earned rewards. The county has much substantial wealth. The face of the country is level, with much prairie, excepting on the water-courses. Cotton is the most important production, and one for which the climate and soil are well suited. Brenham is the county-seat, and quite a thriving place. At this time (1857) there are signs of vigorous improvement, and many new buildings going up; and the ox-wagons, the "peculiar institution" of this country, are hauling away cotton, and returning with merchandise and building materials. The mechanics are all fully employed, and wagons, ploughs, and furniture, are turned out in goodly quantities. The constant din of mechanical sounds, as the rough and stubborn wood and metals are fashioned for the convenience and comfort of man, bespeak a thriving community. The location of Brenham is beautiful; the rolling hills surrounding the town diversify the scenery; and the stately trees, left as Nature planted them, lend a charm to the prospect, and beautify the happy location. A writer says, that the post oak land of this county is much underrated; it is easier cultivated, and fencing cheaper than in the prairie; there is in these lands the advantage of an abundant supply of mast for hogs.

It is estimated that the very few farmers living on the Yeaguas, in this county, sold, during the year 1856, 100,000 pounds of pork, at 4½ to 5 cents per pound. The lands, generally, are noted for their productiveness, readily yielding from 40 to 75 bushels of corn to the acre, or from 1000 to 3000 pounds of cotton.

Improved farms may be purchased at $10 per acre, unimproved land at $3. There is plenty of red-cedar and post-oak timber, and many other less valuable kinds.

Brenham is 100 miles from Galveston.

YOUNG COUNTY.

This is the extreme north-western county in the State, and lies about 350 miles north-west of Austin. It was formed by the legislature of 1856–7, out of Cook county. Fort Belknap and the Indian reservation are within its limits. It is a well watered and timbered county, and a desirable place to live. Following the beaten track from Fort Graham, in Hill county, to Fort Belknap, you will, after a tedious journey through the "Cross Timbers," reach a range of ragged, but open, hills, with the Brazos meandering through the narrow valley. Fort Belknap may be seen in the distance: it is a situation of considerable importance, and has a spacious magazine, comfortable quarters for the troops, and buildings for the officers. Below the fort is a fine spring, and a well of considerable depth, affording abundance of good water. South of the fort, at the distance of half a mile, is the county-seat of Young. In the neighborhood is a bed of bituminous coal, of a superior quality, which, at some future day, will be a valuable product. Following the course of the river about three miles up stream, we find, on the west side, the mouth of Post-oak Creek, with farms in close neighborhood: the creek is about eight or ten miles long, and has a body of land about twelve miles in width, covered with post-oak. On the east side of the river are the Belknap Springs, affording plenty of water for ordinary purposes. Pursuing the river still higher up, we find the mouth of Elm Creek: fertile lands border its banks, which are well timbered: there are half-a-dozen families settled on this creek. A little distance higher up is the mouth of California Creek: here is a beautiful valley of land; only one settler resides in the valley. Six miles further up the Brazos brings the traveler to Boggy Creek: it is of considerable length, fertile soil, and inexhaustible grazing. There are no settlers in this valley. On an elevated point, on the east side of the river, is another of the famous springs of Young county: here is the highest settlement on the river. Taking a northerly course, you ascend the dividing ridge between the head-waters of the Trinity and the valley of the Brazos. From this elevated plateau, the most romantic and enchanting scenery is spread out before the vision: on the one side are seen the numerous little branches of the Trinity, dotted with timber, and, on the other, the vast wilderness of the Brazos valley, stretching far away upon the sight: in other directions, there appears to be no visible terminus of prairie. Here the deer and the antelope freely range, seldom disturbed by the rifles of the white, or the arrows of the red man. The valley of the Brazos, above Fort Belknap, averages between five and six miles wide. It has much good land and timber, sufficient for small farmers and stock-raisers. The highest point of post-oak timber lies about thirty miles above Fort Belknap, where there are many large groves. Here the banks of the Brazos are low: the bed of the river is wide and shallow, and the water becomes quite salt as you ascend. On the high prairie bordering the valley, there is an abundance of mezquit timber, and fine grazing; but it is rather sparingly watered. South and east of Belknap, settlements are sprinkled over the country, at short distances. Salt Creek, running into the Brazos from the east side, and Rock Creek, from the west side, have much post-oak timber on their borders, which afford a plentiful supply of mast for hogs. On Salt Creek there is a good supply of building timber. Following a trail from Fort Belknap, about twelve miles, in a south-eastern direction, over rugged hills, you come to the villages of the Wacos and Tonkaways, upon the "Indian Reservation:" at the distance of a mile is the large trading-house of Charles Barnard, and the residence of the Indian agent. Six miles further, on a beautiful eminence in the bend of the Brazos, you come to the villages of the Delawares, Caddoes, and Shawnees. The Clear Fork of the Brazos is an important stream: its waters run the whole year, and, unlike the Brazos, are sweet to the taste. The valley is already settled as high up as Camp Cooper, and emigrants are coming in daily.

During the year 1856, about 2500 acres of land were under cultivation, in this county. There are several thousand head of stock in the county. The market is good, but limited, at present, to Fort Belknap and Camp Cooper: beeves are worth $13 per head; flour $6 to $8 per cwt.; common laborers $20 per month, and scarce: teams find constant employment, at good rates.

There is every reason to believe that this county abounds in gypsum, coal, iron, and many other minerals, as large lumps of coal, and metallic ores, have been found in the beds of all the streams, and in sinking wells.

CHAPTER IV.

STOCK-RAISING.

THE raising of neat cattle and horses is a business in this State well adapted to persons of small capitals; and men in moderate circumstances, with families, find it very profitable and remunerative employment for their boys, as, at the age of eight or ten, they soon become as efficient as grown hands, and are far more apt in learning.

Boys who are brought up in the stock business become much attached to it, and their interests are generally stimulated by making them the owners of a few head, which, by the time of their majority, are increased to a respectable property, on which to set up for themselves. During the winter months cattle require no attention, thus affording to the youth a period of leisure, for school and study; and, in fact, during the so-called laboring seasons, there is much spare time, which may be employed in the companionship of books. The only drawback which exists to educating the "stock boys," is that the best locations are not usually in neighborhoods where schools are situated. But, under the disadvantage of a lack of schools, the parents, if they possess the inclination, have sufficient time during the year to impart much intellectual instruction to their sons. The employment of cattle-raising is healthful, and imparts muscle, vigor, and agility, to the youthful frame, and forms the constitution for hardship, and the mind for boldness and enterprise, without being in itself hazardous, or even severely laborious. It is invigorating to both body and mind, and models and trains them to manly independence; imparting attributes which are likely to render the possessor a successful combatant in the vicissitudes of life. Stock-raising pays a better per centage, is more certain in profitable results, and requires less risks than any other regular business. It is also a business in which a large or small capital can be employed, with like certainty of success, and not like many others, which cannot be conducted beneficially without vast outlay. It is a business requiring no apprenticeship, and but little skill, and the labor and care are not continuous. It is a business which quickly converts the unclaimed and exhaustless herbage of the wide-spread prairie-commons into money capital, through the quiet instrumentality of the lowing herds. It turns that into property and money which otherwise would return again to the soil, or be blown by the autumn winds away, or melt before the swift fires which sweep over these regions, and leave the earth for miles as bare as before the ages of vegetation. Stock-raising rescues from the elements, and turns the transient herbage into property, and makes it yield employment and support to many persons, and adds wealth and importance to the State.

The Texas prairies, with their never-failing coats of verdure, are alike the property of all for the purposes of pasturage, and those who improve these natural advantages are rescuing from the earth wealth which will go to stimulate the general prosperity.

A stock-raiser commencing business purchases his one or two hundred acres of land, near to, or at the edge of a prairie, and on the border of a creek, spring, or water-course of some kind; for here he can always find timber for his buildings and fences, and protection of the shade trees from the summer sun and northern blasts. Usually these favorite situations are on the outskirts or surroundings of the prairies; but, in many instances, the prairies themselves are interspersed with "*motts*," or "*islands*" of timber, containing from a few rods to many acres; and sometimes they are likewise covered with a growth of majestic live oaks; nevertheless, with this seeming contradiction of terms, these are prairies, there being neither underbrush nor shrub, but the oaks growing singly, and sufficiently near, to shade the ground without deteriorating the grass. A person can ride through them with as little trouble as he can traverse an orchard. Such prairies look to a stranger like grounds which have once been in the keeping of man, and the trees themselves speak of civilized antiquity; but the fresh grass and cheerful aspect lead the wayfarer to expect evidences of settlements; the thought is that civilization has long held dominion, and that Nature, unaided, never arranged such human-like scenery. These natural groves and parks and meadows have no signs about them which the traveller would look for in a recently-settled country, but everything betokens long occupation, without showing any one work made by the hand of man, or mark of his designing. Frequently, in travelling through such scenery, the stranger, despite his better knowledge, is constantly expecting to see the turrets of a baronial castle, or, at least, a sombre brown stone mansion rising among the trees. Often, benighted wayfarers, after a hard day's ride, on coming to such a region, are sadly disappointed in their calculations about refreshments; and, during the tedious vigils of the night, as they lie camped, with no cover but the canopy of Heaven, do they ever and anon prick up their ears to an imaginary cock-crow or dog-bark, when perhaps there is not a domestic animal, save their own jaded mule, within a hundred miles. This scenery is grand and majestic, yet chaste, beautiful, and harmonious as the Garden of our Forefathers.

Some of the large prairies have very few islands of timber, or trees, or brush of any kind, and a person near the centre can only see a low, dim line of misty green, which is the timber on the water-courses, that define and bound the prairies. Sometimes the limits are beyond the vision, and the traveller beholds a boundless ocean of grass, here and there dotted with dark spots, indicative of small timber islands, which agreeably relieve the sameness. These islands are frequently signs of springs, or of a greater degree of moisture near the surface. The streams and water-courses, which bound the prairies, all have bottoms of greater or less extent, which are covered on either side with heavy growths of timber; and again, beyond the bottoms, those natural meadows commence; but the timber and shrubbery are continually encroaching on them from every side, and diminishing, year by year, their area; roads, cow-paths, and water-gullies, tend to isolate small tracts, and thereby foster and protect the foresters from the devouring element, fire, which is their scourge; but, in time, this process will convert the prairies into woodland. Near the seaboard, the prairies are of the most uniform surface and greatest extent. A man journeying over one becomes astonished at the magnificent grandeur of their proportions, and is much dissatisfied with his own puny efforts at progress; the straining eye becomes sated and tired with the sameness, and longs for a hill or precipice, or some other natural deformity, wherewith to be diverted.

When the stock-raiser has made his selection, the first business is to build a pen, for the herding of his cattle, and then a small log or frame house, covered with oak-boards; next, he fences in a few acres of the rich prairie, for the culture of his corn and garden "*stuff;*" as he expresses it, "makes a patch

6 *

large enough to bread his family." And, in truth, all the space that this family, with their stock, will occupy, out of the whole prairie before them, is but a patch; and hundreds of other patches might be appropriated, without apparently diminishing the great whole. The cattle-raiser supplies himself with two or three Mexican horses, for herding, a few hogs, and other domestic animals; and, having a small stock of cattle, no family, with moderate means, can, under any other circumstances, begin so soon to feel independent of the world, for all the comforts of life.

In commencing, it would be best to purchase one hundred head of cows, with their calves, and two or three bulls. A stock started in this way remains more gentle, and are not so apt to stray, as an average stock: they can be purchased, in this way, for $10 the cow and calf. The increase is very rapid, and soon outnumbers the highest calculations of the sanguine owner. The stock require very little attention, excepting in the spring and fall: in March, the herding and marking and branding the young calves are performed: where there are many stocks commingled, in one range, the owners club together, and drive herds of one or two hundred into a pen, when each owner singles out his calves, ropes and brands them. This herding is continued until all but a few scattering ones are gone through with. In the fall season, when the weather becomes cool, the herding, marking, branding, and altering, are again done, in the same way: this time includes all the stragglers left at any previous branding, and all that have been dropped since spring. In a small stock, whose range is near no other, so that the owner has to depend for its management on his own force, it is deemed best to be frequently among them, and to mark, brand, and alter the calves as soon as they are old enough, always having regard to the proper seasons. This keeps the stock more tractable, and familiarizes them with man; and the owners soon come to know every animal in the herd, and one cannot get astray without being missed. Stocks of cattle will thrive and increase, with very little care and attention; but it is found, from experience, that the bestowal of a considerable degree of attention on them is well remunerated, and that they become more docile.

There is always a demand for beef and stock cattle: men come here, and buy up large droves of the latter, for the Missouri and Illinois farmers, and California rancheros: in those places, the cattle are more valuable than in Texas. Many beef-cattle are shipped from here to New Orleans, and much of the regular supply for said city comes from Texas. Indianola, on Matagorda bay, is the principal shipping-port for cattle. There are several persons, at that place, who make regular shipments, every week, by the steamers. Galveston and Corpus Christi have participated in this trade, but many more beeves are shipped from Matagorda bay than all other ports. The high value of hides, for the last year, has added much to the profits of the stock-raiser. They used to be thought hardly worth saving, and, when saved, the stretching and curing was so carelessly performed, that very little was received for them: of late, a better economy has dictated more care; and our hides, which are really of extra quality intrinsically, are becoming quite an article of commerce. During our war with Mexico, I have seen thirty beeves killed, every other day, to supply the army, and the hides thrown to the vultures.

Steers, at three and four years old, are considered beeves; and are sold to contractors, who ship them to New Orleans, or to the planters here. The value of four-year-olds is about $15. The stock-raisers who have families, generally, during the spring and summer months, have their pens full of milch-cows, from each of which they take but little milk, and are continually turning out and replenishing their yards from the prairies. The calves of the milking-cows are kept up, so long as their dams are required; and they and the milker divide the products of the udder, the calves getting the greatest share. Large quantities of butter and cheese might be made by the stock-raisers; but an improvident neglect in our people allows those articles to be imported from abroad, in large quantities — foreign butter, in the winter, frequently selling at fifty cents per pound, and cheese at twenty-five cents.

The term "stock-cattle" is conventional, and means, in five hundred head, the following proportions, viz.:

170 cows, with their calves,
65 steer-calves, under one year old,
65 heifer-calves, under one year old,
55 two-year-old steers,
55 two-year-old heifers,
45 three-year-old steers,
45 three-year-old heifers;

making 500 head, of all varieties. And such a stock of cattle is worth $2500, or at the rate of $5 per head. The selling price per head does not vary, whether the stock be large or small. There are laws requiring every stock-owner to adopt a mark and brand different from any of his neighbors, and to have the same recorded in the county clerks office. The criminal laws have several provisions for the protection of stock owners' rights against dishonest persons: there is also an estray-law, which obliges the taker-up of a strange animal to give sufficient publicity.

The cattle of this State have never been subject to any endemical, epidemical, or contagious diseases, to make the business of stock-raising precarious and uncertain; and very few die, excepting the old cows—these generally live to the age of twenty years, and frequently have calves the last year. However, the inclement winter of 1855–6 was extremely disastrous to stock of all kinds, and even to wild animals: in Texas, it is estimated that at least twenty-five per cent. of all the neat cattle in the State died from the effects of cold: some of the older States are said to have lost over fifty per cent., from the same cause; but such a season was never before experienced. Thousands of cattle, in good order, became so paralyzed with intense cold, that they dropped down while feeding, and perished where they fell. During all of the fall of 1855, and the fore part of the winter, the weather was genial and warm, like spring: the annual trees leaved out, and many blossomed, and the prairies were clothed with the newest and brightest green, mingled with tender-painted wild-flowers of every hue: fig-bushes were loaded, and the fruit ripened; and the contented stock were basking in a paradise of rich, juicy herbage; but, about Christmas, a change came over this scene, and the face of Nature, which so recently had glowed with tropical verdure, was, by a sudden change of temperature, metamorphosed into a Siberian aspect — the green was all wilted, withered, sered, and turned to sombre brown; and, from the previous superabundance of graminivorous food, the stock-cattle became reduced to *old fog*. This extreme cold commenced on the 24th day of December, 1855, and ended about the 1st of March, 1856. The greatest cold, on the coast, was 15° below the freezing-point; and, as 18° is the point that kills annual vegetation, every kind of prairie herbage was soon dead. Grass was all destroyed, at that early date; and about seven weeks elapsed before any signs of spring were seen, and all of March passed before much food could be obtained for the thousands of starving cattle: the dead grass of the prairies had undergone a baneful chemical change, by the action of frost; and it had not only lost its nutritive qualities, but was positively injurious; and, opening the animals that died, their stomachs were found full of undigested rubbish. Old cows, and bulls of all ages, suffered most; yearlings next; and, after these latter, even yearlings whose dams had not been milked the previous summer, seemed little able to bear the severity. Cattle that were sheltered from the cold winds suffered as much as those left to themselves, in the open prairies — though the sufferings of the former were more from want of food than from cold. The seaboard counties, and all of that region of country lying west of the Colorado, are well adapted to stock-raising; but the coast counties are preferable to the interior: the former combine many advantages, the prairies being larger than in the interior, winters shorter, and the grass continues good the whole year, the heat of summer being tempered by the delightful breezes of the Gulf of Mexico, and at no time is the weather on the prairie oppressive.

Another great advantage to a large stock-raiser is, that shipping depots are handy, from any point in those counties, and agents are constantly scouring the country, gathering in beeves for New Orleans. Matagorda and Jackson counties I think preferable to any others, and the prairies of Trespalacios and Karankawa are certainly unsurpassed in the requisites for this business.

The best shipping place for the coast country is the town of Palacios, which has hereinbefore been referred to. It is the most natural and convenient place, for the crafts which navigate the Colorado, to load and discharge at: here the deep water and firm land are in close proximity; and good roads can be stretched out to the interior, in every direction.

There are many desirable situations for stock-raisers and small farmers along the Trespalacios and its spring tributaries.

It will be seen, by the comptroller's report, that some of the interior counties have many more cattle than any of those on the seaboard; but it must also be recollected, that the area of the former is many times greater. There is now one young man living on the Trespalacios who has a stock of 10,000 head!

There is one important matter which the people of Texas have almost wholly neglected, viz., an improvement of their cattle, by importing superior stock from abroad: through this oversight or parsimony, our stocks have suffered much deterioration, in the qualities most desired.

Steers from the Texas prairies make very good work oxen, are tractable and easily broken: they are much used by the planters and farmers, in the cultivation of their crops, and in hauling the same to market. The Texas cattle are descendants, with few crosses, from the old Mexican stocks, and they are well adapted to the country: still, where the breed has been crossed by better stock, the offspring are superior, and thrive well.

As I before remarked, our cattle have many good traits: the steers are easily broken, and gentle treatment will overcome the wildest: they are never vicious, but extremely tractable when taken out of the prairie.

The usual practice of farmers, whenever they want work oxen, is to go to the prairie, and neck together, with ropes, as many pair of three and four-year-old steers as they desire: these, in the course of a week or so, can be yoked to the draught. I have seen boys thirteen years old ploughing with three yokes of these oxen, holding the plough, and managing their teams with nothing but a small whip.

CHAPTER V.

SHEEP—HONEY-BEES.

SHEEP-RAISERS, in Texas, have not, as a general thing, been successful, excepting on the islands and peninsulas along the coast. In all probability, the failures have been more owing to want of proper attention, than to any innate defect of herbage or climate.

The Mexican stocks that have been introduced to these localities have universally kept healthy, improved in the fleece, and multiplied exceedingly fast. Horses and mules are raised, with as little trouble and expense as cattle, in all parts of the State. The native stock, with a heavier cross, makes the best offspring for service and endurance; and they will maintain themselves in good condition, on the prairies, winter and summer, and only require the additional feed of a few ears of corn, when continually worked. The prairies were all, in former times, well stocked with wild horses, or *mustangs;* and they still range in those prairies where they have not been too much disturbed. Many of these animals are of remarkable symmetry of body and limb, and equal in speed and bottom to the Arab *barb.*

Only a few years have elapsed since there was a large drove of those animals that ranged on the Matagorda prairie; and two of the finest of the males were caught, after running and counter-running 600 or 700 miles, breaking down several relays of horses and riders. A fine breed of horses has sprung from one of these animals.

HONEY-BEES.

These insects have not been extensively cultivated, but sufficiently so to show that they are worth the attention of farmers. The trees, shrubs, and flowers of Texas are never-failing sources for these industrious producers; and they require no attention, excepting at swarming time, and to gather the sweets of their silent labors: here, too, they are very seldom afflicted with vermin and insects, and thrive best when left to their own way. Every family may, without cost, have its twenty, thirty, or a hundred hives, and make it a source of profit, pleasure, and gratification.

The forests are full of wild bees, and every old hollow tree is filled with well-stored cells; and this is the case even in the vicinities of long and thickly settled communities: very little pleasant trouble will always insure an abundance of wild honey, during the proper season. Any one can furnish himself with a stock of bees, by hiving the swarms of wild ones, in the spring, as they migrate from the paternal domicil. Wild bees become domestic, and produce well. I have seen 350 hives of bees in the front-yard of one cottage, standing on the ground: in summer time, when the whole upper world was full of them, it was like running the gauntlet, to get to the house. The production of these hives was a nice income for the owner: his wax was shipped to New York, and the honey was put up in casks, and sent to the seaboard towns, where it always found ready purchasers. I suppose the net proceeds were not less than $1000 per annum. Thus can the prudent man, in a new country, make subservient to his profit and comfort the boons of Nature, which, without foresight, would be wasted on the desert air: he can greatly relieve from his shoulders the curse which is inherited from our original parents.

CHAPTER VI.

WHEAT.

THIS important grain has only been cultivated a few years in Texas; and, in fact, that portion of the State best adapted to it was but yesterday an uninhabited wilderness. The best wheat region is above the line of 32° north. I learn that there is much of the last year's crop on hand, which, for want of facilities of getting to market, is not at present a very remunerative crop. Farmers bring wheat to Austin from a distance of 200 miles, and also to Houston, a distance of over 300 miles; and hauling back freights makes the business pay; but nothing, in comparison, is netted to the farmer, that would be, if there were railroads.

However great the discouragements labored under, they have, by their energy, tested the qualities of our soil, and practically demonstrated that all of the northern part of Texas is pre-eminently a superior wheat country. And, I would ask, if, with all the drawbacks which the wheat-raisers now are subject to, they have been able to profitably succeed, what will be the wonderful results, when good merchant-mills are established, and railroad communication extends from the coast, through the planting sections, to the wheat region?

Northern Texas can supply all the balance of the State with good superfine flour, and successfully compete with the Western States in the New Orleans market. We have the soil and climate for wheat, and only require the stimulus of proper inducements to bring its culture into extensive operation.

The following is the wheat crop of twenty-five counties, for the year 1856, viz:

Counties.	Bushels.
Burnett	10,000
Cass	28,000
Cherokee	20,000
Colin	130,000
Cook	20,000
Coryell	15,000
Dallas	150,000
Denton	10,000
Ellis	50,000
El Paso	100,000
Fannin	125,000
Grayson	100,000
Henderson	25,000
Hill	20,000
Hopkins	50,000
Hunt	50,000
Johnson	30,000
Kaufman	60,000
Lamar	150,000
McLellan	30,000
Navarro	30,000
Red River	100,000
Tarrant	40,000
Upshur	20,000
Williamson	25,000
Total	2,183,000

There are seventy counties in the State which produced wheat last year (1856).

The "State Gazette," a reliable newspaper, published at Austin, says the citizens of Colin County are furnishing Fort Washita with flour at the low price of $2·75 per cwt., or about $5·50 per bbl. New wheat has been selling, in the wheat-growing counties, during the last winter, for 50 cents per bushel. It is only a year or so since the farmers in the foregoing counties commenced raising wheat; and, indeed, it is but a short time ago since those counties were undefined and uninhabited regions of wilderness.

The wheat culture, as yet, is only an experiment, conducted without the proper appliances, and to the greatest disadvantage; but still, enough has been done to conclusively demonstrate that wheat is destined to be the most valuable production of this State. All of the counties north of 31° can depend on wheat as a certain crop.

CHAPTER VII.

CREDIT.

Credit, in Texas, is the universal rule, and prompt payment the exception; the system runs through all business, from the smallest account to the most important contract.

The doctor, the lawyer, the editor, the merchant, mechanic, and undertaker, all furnish their wares on credit, and so we live and pass through life, and finally die on tick.

During the Republic, and particularly in the latter days thereof, people became apparently very poor in the circulating medium. All kinds of property were very much depreciated; land and stock-cattle had no convertible cash values; business transactions became very limited between the citizens, and nearly all their trade was carried on in barter, and the exchange of commodities; and in the sales of property and effects, on credit, to be paid for, at some future time, in other property. Having little commerce and connection by trade with foreign countries, that promptness and certainty which is the life and soul of regular business, were lost sight of, and a disregard to the fulfilment of promises became general. Thus, a man purchased of his neighbor, under a solemn promise to make payment in a given time, predicating his obligation on the faith of promises made by others to him, which, of course, failed; he was necessarily not punctual, because others disappointed him; his neighbor could not fulfil his duties to others, because his means, on which such duties were predicated, were in the hands of his debtors. And the ramifications of debt, credit, bad faith, broken contracts, and disappointed calculations, became the general rule of society. Cattle and horses were good conventional representatives of value, but land was not current, and the possessor of an over-quantity was impoverished by the taxes on a species of property which possessed no real active market value. Men became disregardful of all punctuality in their contracts, because others broke their words to them; if a negligent debtor had not acted exactly as he had agreed, he was no worse than people generally around him, and no one thought him a worse man. Careless indifference for the moral obligation of all contracts became so general, that even those who had the means of promptly paying their debts, found it hard to belie the ruling fashion. Every person used the privilege of running in debt to the extent of his or her ability of doing so.

On the formation of our State Constitution, it was hoped that some kind of a banking system would be legalized, but the *democratic* wisdom of the members of the Convention who manufactured our Constitution, would not for an instant entertain such an enormity as a banking law. They forgot that we were to become an important agricultural and commercial people; that our exports and imports would, in a few years, become extensive; that a business medium of exchange, after the fashion of other civilized communities, would be required; and if we could not have it of our own, our necessities would force us to contribute to the prosperity of neighboring States, for the use of their banking paper. The *barbaric* restrictions in our Constitution against banks, have obstructed all of our commercial transactions with the people of other States, and been the fostering cause, at home, of all the evils of a loose credit system. Our *fathers*, in their enthusiastic regard for *hard currency*, overlooked the salutary and invigorating results of a good banking system; they had been too long isolated from the busy concerns and interests of the trading world to legislate intelligently for a young and thriving nation. They seemed to have forgotten that a safe banking system is, in all ages, the balance-wheel, which regulates all business relations of society, and causes the people to be prudent, prompt, and reliable, in all their dealings; that establishes punctuality between man and man, promotes the morals of society, conduces to fair dealing, and makes it not only dishonorable, but unprofitable, for any man to forfeit his word or his bond. The people of Texas, under their new ægis of a State Government, not having the proper constraints, examples, and incentives, did not reform, to any noticeable degree, their old habits of running in debt; and when the agricultural wealth of our country began to be developed, and to create commercial business with foreign States, and the merchandise and productions of other people were attracted here for a market, the credit system continued; the merchants sold on credit, and the planters and farmers, mechanics and citizens, bought on credit; and so it continues, throughout all classes, to this day. Old habits are hard to be rid of, without some powerful influence to the contrary; and the accessions of population from abroad, instead of tending to a reformation, easily fall into the customs of the country.

All merchants' accounts for goods sold to the inhabitants during the year, are considered due on the following first of January. Those that are not paid at that date are generally closed by promissory note, bearing ten per cent. interest from date, and made payable one day after date; and frequently, when an account is settled in this manner, the merchant also charges 2½ per cent. for advancing. He can make no calculation on getting in his debts at any particular time; and often, after long and vexatious delays, rendered doubly annoying by the constant reception of polite notes from his friends in New York and New Orleans, he is obliged to sue; this, even if he saves the whole of his debt, is at a cost of ten per cent., to be paid to his lawyer. Some portion of the amount credited out by the merchant, during the year, is certain to be totally lost in bad debts; and all of these losses, of course, are taken into consideration in regulating his scale of profits. The merchants who go into the great marts to purchase their stocks of goods, under the disadvantages of the reputation of being slow and uncertain paymasters, are forced to pay much higher prices than a more prompt class. Therefore, the New York merchant who sells to the Texan merchant, knowing the precarious business of his customer, puts on to the price his profit accordingly, to cover interest on uncertain time of payment, and a liberal charge as insurance for probable losses and ultimate litigation. The Texan, in order to prosper, must, and does, when he sells his goods, charge his profits on the exhorbitant prices which he has paid; and, like the New Yorker, he, too, charges his extras in the way of interest on long time, and an insurance against the probable average of bad debts. And all of this accumulated load of charges has to be borne by the consumers; they are the real sufferers. Besides, the blandishments of an easy credit system are very liable to lead its votaries to embarrassment and ultimate ruin. Thus the farmers' and planters' families, who have unlimited credit at the neighboring stores during the year, purchase many more goods than they would if credit were abolished; they are not prudent with what they do get, and they pay more than cash values, and thereby their expenses are enhanced, and accumulating debts created.

When brief credit accommodates the necessities of

prudent persons, it is beneficial; but, when it ministers to the imperative calls of extravagance, its effects are destructive.

Our merchants, with a few exceptions, are inexperienced young men when they commence business, whose capital consists of the letters of recommendation, which they obtain from responsible persons, and take, in place of more substantial substance, to the commercial cities of the North. These are used, instead of money, in the purchase of stocks of goods, to be sold out in Texas. Purchases made under such great disadvantages, too frequently cause our merchants to be unsuccessful in business; they often are forced, after a precarious existence of two or three years, amid the constant vexations of duns from their creditors abroad, and forfeited promises from their debtors at home, to close up, with broken spirits, frustrated expectations, and ruined reputations, to the heavy loss of their too facile creditors. Thus, in many instances, have honest young men been ruined by the great facilities afforded for getting stocks of goods, and becoming merchants. As this is a portion of the credit system, and comes into the general account of losses, our consumers, the Texan planters, farmers, and stock-raisers, have its incidents to pay for in the way of high prices on all the articles which they purchase. The system of credit has made goods more expensive, in Texas, than they otherwise would be; and if a few solitary consumers pay cash for their merchandise, they still, under the present state

8

of affairs, must pay to the merchant charges which were predicated on the credit system. The whole system is a wrong, and vitally injurious to the consumer. Men totally unsuited for merchants get goods too easily, and the merchants of New York, and other large cities, are too willing to sell, and too slow to discriminate between their customers. Young men are very apt to misjudge their capacities, and to entertain a false notion about the different occupations of life; it has become a current sentiment, that the selling of merchandise confers a gentlemanly distinction, while the honest vocation of cultivating the earth is considered only adapted to rustic grovellers.

In a new country, fast settling with emigration from older States, short credite are useful, and frequently absolutely necessary, to enable the settler to get along for a year or two; for, most generally, they are men of limited means, and the whole of it is required in the purchase of lands and stock animals; they must have many things which they cannot bring with them, and, for such necessaries, a credit at the neighboring stores is useful; but, after the first two or three years, no more credit should be required, or, if indulged in, it ought to be short, and promptly wiped out, either by money, or by cotton, corn, hides, or other productions. The merchants of New York, and other cities, who sell for the Texas trade, should only entrust their goods to those persons who have ample tangible capital, or who give undoubted security on property in Texas; and then, if men *will* undertake mercantile business without proper capacity, the losses by their ruin will not have to be paid for by the Texan consumers. I have frequently known men to contract debts, in New York, of $20,000 yearly, without giving any security, and who could not, had they not in possession such goods, so bought on credit of strangers, have purchased, in Texas, $500 worth of property on a credit, without giving security. Let the New York merchants look more to the security of their business transactions, and the quickness and certainty of their returns; let them take such precautions, that losses shall not be possible; let them do only what any ordinary man, in any ordinary business transaction, considers necessary, to wit: make proper security paramount, make prompt payment an object of primary importance, and the Texas trade would become established on a firmer basis, and the consumers would become more prosperous and better producers. Let the consumers eschew credit, for it is the incubus of their lives, the moth which secretly destroys their substance.

The productions of Texas, which are suitable for foreign markets, are abundant and numerous, such as cotton, sugar, hides, beeswax, and wool, and far superior in value to all the merchandise which we require from abroad; these are every year increasing; but, instead of being of full benefit to the producers, much of their values are frittered away by the enormous expenses of the credit system. Credit, at best, is subserviency to a hard master; and, when the people become so lost to their own interests as to adopt credit altogether, the springs of their prosperity are directed into improper channels, and the resources of the producer are consumed in paying for curses rather than blessings.

CHAPTER VIII.

SCHOOLS.

THE people of Texas have, by princely munificence, laid the foundation of a general system of education. This subject has been well considered, and has received the particular attention of every successive legislature, since annexation.

To diffuse the means of education throughout the land, and to bring it near the door of every habitation, without cost to the recipient, will be the ultimate effect of these wise provisions. During the Republic of Texas, Congress appropriated four leagues of land (or 17,712 acres) to every county, for educational purposes, and every new county receives the like amount of land: besides, the constitution of the State has provided, that no less than one-tenth of the annual State-tax shall be set apart for purposes of education; which money passes to the credit of the common-school fund, and is held inviolably sacred for that purpose.

By a law of 1854, the sum of $2,000,000, of the five per cent. U. S. bonds, was also set apart for a *special* school-fund; and, by a law of 1856, the same was blended with the money derivable from the tenth of the taxes, and the whole is made a general school-fund: the interest derivable from all school moneys is appropriated annually for schools. Our State being large, and sparsely settled, has prevented, as yet, the school system from going into general practical effect. By a recent enactment, each county has been laid off into common-school districts, and a certain portion of the school-fund is to be divided among the several counties, according to the number of children from six to sixteen years of age. The tuition of poor children is first to be provided for out of the appropriation, and the balance is divided *pro rata* among the other scholars. It is not presumed that this money will be sufficient to pay the whole year's tuition, in any one district, but it will go far in educating the poor. The lands, together with the increasing fund, must, under ordinary circumstances, place the means of education within the reach of every child in the State. Both during the Republic and under the State government, much public land has been granted, in fee simple, to institutions of learning, aside from the general grants. Institutions so endowed are scattered throughout the older parts of the State; and, with increasing renown and importance, they are, year by year, nurturing up males and females in the paths of virtue and high intellectual development. Schools, academies, churches, and newspapers, are sure guarantees of liberty to the people; for, where education, religion, and knowledge are general, none but just laws can be made; a proper regard will be observed for the rights of all; justice, correct principles, and our republican institutions, will be sustained, and tyranny repelled by united force. A few years, and a few more thousand emigrants, will ripen and perfect our school system, and make our valuable lands available for all the noble ends and purposes intended. And, even now, the want of a good English education, by the very poorest of the rising generation, will be more attributable to criminal neglect, or want of natural capacity, than to a lack of the means. Emigrants from the older States, who have children, need not fear that the privileges of schools will be left behind; for they can settle in almost any county in the State, and still enjoy all the blessings of a refined and cultivated civilization. Schools, churches, and newspapers, the concomitants of well-organized society, are accessible and convenient to every community, and a very superior degree of general intelligence distinguishes this people above any of the new States of the Union.

Sixty-four newspapers are published in this State: far more, it is true, than pay well; but the ability and intelligence displayed in their columns, show that really good editors can subsist on very short commons. We already have men of eminence in all the walks of literature and science, and public libraries and lyceums have been established in all the towns.

CHAPTER IX.

TAXATION, AND HOW IT AFFECTS THE OWNERS OF PROPERTY.

THE rate of taxation is fifteen cents on each hundred dollars' valuation of real and personal property. There are excepted from taxation two hundred and fifty dollars' worth of household furniture, or other personal property, to each family.

County taxes may be one-half of the State-tax, but shall not exceed that rate.

For the years 1854–5–6–7, nine-tenths of all the State-tax has been relinquished to the respective counties in which the taxed property is situate, and the remaining tenth of said tax goes to the credit of the common-school fund. Persons owning property must make out their assessment list, and hand it to the assessor and collector of taxes, between January and May of each year.

Property situate in any county in the State can be given in, and taxes paid in any other county.

Taxes become due on the first of October of each year, and are payable at any time between that and the following first of March.

TO PERSONS WHO OWN LANDS IN TEXAS, AND HAVE NEGLECTED TO PAY TAXES.

All lands which have not, in years past, been regularly given in for assessment and taxation, have been *assessed as non-residents' property*, and sold for taxes and costs. All such lands have either been purchased by individuals, or bid in by the State. By a law passed Feb. 5, 1856, the owners of such lands, so bid off by the State, may redeem the same by paying to the assessor and collector where the land lies, or to the comptroller, at Austin, all arrearages of unpaid taxes, with fifty per cent. per annum on all the taxes that are or *should* be due on such lands up to time of payment, and two dollars fee, over and above the other charges. When land is purchased by an individual, at tax-sale, the deed of the assessor and collector, provided it be regularly recorded in the proper office, becomes, according to law, *prima facie* evidence of title in the purchaser; provided, further, that the person whose property has been sold for taxes, shall have two years to redeem the same, by paying to such assessor, or to the purchaser, double the amount of taxes, with costs of sale. All lands not rendered in for taxation, are valued and assessed by the assessor, according to the average valuation of all the land in the counties where situate.

ADVICE TO NON-RESIDENTS OWNING LANDS IN TEXAS.

You see, by the foregoing laws, that if your property here is not attended to, it will inevitably be sold for the taxes; and that, if not bid in by the State, you stand a fair chance of having it sacrificed to the cupidity of some wily speculator, or of recovering it only at the termination of an expensive law-suit — a hazard which should not be run by any man who has any regard for his own welfare. It is true, that, in the States of Ohio and Illinois, where the greatest number of tax-sales have been made, and the most tax-titles have been tested in the courts, few have withstood the ordeal: it is said that only twenty-five, out of many hundreds, have been sustained; still, it is suicidal policy to trust one's property to the chances of law.

Only two or three tax-cases have been decided by our courts of last resort, and those went against the tax purchasers; but, I suppose, at an expense to the winner of nearly the value of the property recovered. The cases decided will be no inducement or argument for tax purchasers to give up their acquisitions easily; for the reason, that each tax purchase rests for its validity on its own peculiar circumstances. If the preliminaries to the sale, and the sale and concomitants, have been done and observed according to law, then the tax-sale becomes a perfect title, and fully vests the property, after two years.

If you have lands in Texas, and no attention has been given to them, for several years, be assured that they have, ere this, been sold for taxes; and, if worth owning, in all probability passed into the hands of speculating individuals, who are ever on the alert to take advantage of the neglectful and unwary, and to profit by the misfortunes of others. And, if your lands are quite valuable, at present or in prospective, such tax purchasers, knowing the liability of their titles to inherent defects, will fortify by actual possession. Our laws of limitation are short; and a defective title, with possession, is quickly ripened into a perfect title.

Thus, lands which are valuable and constantly appreciating, are yearly passing from the rightful owners to the proprietorship of avaricious speculators; or, if they do not wholly and entirely pass, are becoming so entrammelled by the meshes of adverse interests, that recovery will hardly pay the expense.

In order to maintain and hold your lands intact, free from embarrassments, or cloud of controversy, you must cause your titles to be recorded in the county where each respective tract is situate, and have a reliable agent here, to give in your lands for assessment, by *proper descriptions*, and pay taxes on the same; for which services you should pay, in order that it may be obligatory on him to preserve your interests; for the good reason, that services not remunerated are but poorly performed.

You will be amply rewarded for your small expense, by the security which such a course will afford to your property: you will purchase peace of mind, and exemption from trouble and litigation, at a cheap rate.

The lands of Texas are of far more value and consideration than they were during our separate sovereignty; and many a man who is now neglecting his Texas lands, will, in a few years, appear as ridiculous as Esau.

Those persons of the masculine gender, and of mature age, owning lands in Texas, who cunningly say to themselves, "My land, in that benighted region, is all safe: it costs nothing to keep it, for I pay no taxes; and, when the country settles up, and railroads begin to travel that way, I'll be *thar* for a big spec." True it is, your lands will be pretty much in *statu quo*, so far as their area and depth are concerned; but the transmutable part will have departed from you and your heirs. And what's the pity? Shall it be for any man to evade payment of his just quota towards the government? Shall roads be laid out through the wilds at the exclusive expense of residents? Shall school-houses and churches be erected, and the country converted from a wilderness to a populous State, to the *non-resident non-tax-payer's* pecuniary benefit, and without one cent of his aid? It is an injury to any State or country, for *non-residents* to own its territory: then, of course, it is short of justice that they should not pay taxes on their lands, like those who are citizens. But there are many persons, living in the older States, who are of the gentler sex, or of immature years, who own much land in Texas, by inheritance—whose husbands, fathers, brothers, or other kindred, won the right, by their strong arms and ready wills, during our Revolution — who sacrificed money, time, and health in the cause of our liberties, and even laid down their lives, amid wretchedness and suffering, that we might enjoy in peace this beautiful heritage. Towards such land-owners the law would be merciful, if it could discriminate; and it is much to be regretted that they too must suffer; they in whose veins perhaps courses the family blood that bedewed the same lands which they have inherited.

To all such I will say, although you be of weak age or of the gentler sex, or bowed with poverty, suffer not one moment to lapse between yourself and an investigation of your rights; address some reliable agent in Texas, setting forth the known or supposed grounds of your claim, and ask to have it looked into without delay; this can be done void of expense, and, if your rights have been long neglected, you can always get them attended to for a contingent fee in money or in kind. Your journeying to Texas is wholly unnecessary, for you might travel about in this country of high charges and long roads for a year, and be no better informed than when you came; and when, too, perhaps, an agent might do all your business in half the time it would take you to come here.

In conclusion, I will repeat to you, all who have rights in Texas, employ a *trusty agent*, and you will find it to your interest; for titles to real estate, as you must already understand, are not held in the same sacred, inviolable regard, as in England, and owners become more easily divested than in many of the older States.

CHAPTER X.

HEIRSHIP, AND RIGHTS TO PROPERTY BY INHERITANCE.

Law of March 18th, 1848—*Vol. II., page* 129.

This law is now in force, and from its peculiarly equitable provisions, will undoubtedly continue to be the law of the land for many years hence. I have herein inserted a synopsis of it for the particular benefit and reference of those persons living in other States, and having inheritances in Texas.

I have also annexed forms for proving up *heirships*, as I find that people at a distance, and even high *functionaries*, who are expected to be well informed about the laws, usually make blunders. The heirs of persons who died previous to 18th December, 1837, inherit according to Spanish law; that is, first descendants; if they fail, second ascendants; if they fail, third collaterals.

The laws, previous to 1848, are not materially variant.

Law of March 18th, 1848.

1. A person dying without a *will*, and leaving no surviving husband nor wife, the property descends to the children in equal proportions.

2. If there be no children, then to the descendants of the children.

3. If there be no children nor descendants, then to the father and mother of the deceased person, in equal portions.

4. If there be only one of the *parents* of the deceased person surviving, then the inheritance is to be divided into two equal parts, one of which passes to such surviving parent, and the other passes to the brothers and sisters of such deceased person, or to the descendants of them.

5. If the deceased leave only one parent surviving, but no brothers or sisters, nor descendants of brothers or sisters, then such surviving parent inherits the whole.

6. If the deceased person leave no parent surviving, but leave brothers and sisters, or the descendants of such, then all of the inheritance shall pass to such brothers and sisters, or their descendants.

7. If both parents be dead, and there be neither brother nor sister, nor their descendants, then the inheritance is divided into two equal parts, one part of which goes to the paternal, and the other to the maternal kindred of the deceased person, in the following manner, that is to say: the grandfathers and grandmothers in equal proportions; but if only one paternal or maternal grandparent survive, such survivor takes the whole of one moiety.

8. If both grandparents, on either or both sides, be dead, then the inheritance passes to uncles, or to

their nearest lineal descendants; always recollecting, that when there are no legal heirs up to grandparents, the estate is then divided into two equal parts, and one portion goes to the kin of the mother of the deceased, and the other to the kin of the father.

9. When a person, owning property in his or her own right, dies intestate, leaving a surviving husband or surviving wife, and children, or descendants of children, the surviving husband or wife takes one-third of the personal estate, and an estate for life in one-third of the land and slaves, with remainder to the surviving children, or their descendants. The children, or their descendants, inherit the whole of the land and slaves, subject to the life-incumbrance on one-third. They also inherit the other two-thirds of the personal estate.

10. If the deceased leave no children, nor their descendants, but leave a surviving wife or husband, then the surviving husband or wife inherits all the personal estate, and one half of the lands and slaves, without remainder to any person.

11. If the deceased husband or wife left neither children, father nor mother, nor surviving brothers or sisters, or their descendants, then the surviving husband or wife inherits the whole estate.

12. Where an inheritance passes by law to brothers and sisters, if part of such be of the whole blood, and part of the half blood, then, in that case, the half blood inherits half as much as the whole blood.

13. Where the children of the deceased person's

brothers and sisters come into the partition, they take *per capita;* where a part are dead, and a part living, the issue of those dead take *per stirpes.* In this manner, suppose a man die, leaving two surviving brothers or sisters, and the children of a deceased brother or sister, then the surviving brothers or sisters would take *per capita,* and the children of the deceased brother or sister would take *per stirpes,* or the *stock* of their deceased parent.

14. Bastards, whose parents afterwards marry, become, if recognised, legitimated.

MARITAL RIGHTS.

Separate Property — Common Property.

1. Females marrying under the age of twenty-one shall be deemed of full age.

2. All property owned by husband or wife before marriage, and that acquired afterwards by gift, devise, or descent, and the increase of all lands and slaves thus acquired, shall be and continue his or her own separate property.

3. During the marriage, the husband has the sole management of the separate property of the wife.

4. A married woman cannot make separate contracts, by which she herself, or her separate property, will be rendered liable, excepting in cases of absolute necessity for the preservation of her property, or the support of herself and family, and when the husband refuses to join.

5. All property acquired after the marriage, by

either husband or wife, or both, excepting that in Sect. 2, is community or *common* property of the husband and wife; and on the dissolution of the marriage by death, one half goes to the surviving husband or wife, and the other half to their children; but, if they have no children, then the surviving husband or wife takes the whole.

6. After the wife commences a suit for divorce, the husband can contract no further debts, binding on the community property, nor dispose of any land or slaves.

7. All head-right certificates and military land claims, the rights to which have accrued to married men, are considered community property, and governed, in their descent, according to the foregoing laws.

Forms for proving up Heirship.

Suppose a single man, who died in Texas, has connections in the State of New York, and that his father and mother are also dead.

"STATE OF NEW YORK, SS. }
Madison County. }

"Before me, the undersigned, legally constituted authority, personally appeared Samuel Slyke and Jonathan Barlow, two credible witnesses, to me personally well known, who, after being duly sworn, according to law, depose and say, that they are well acquainted with James Parkins, Rufus Parkins, and Sarah Tilton (formerly Parkins), and now wife of

Thomas Tilton; who are all residents of Madison county, in the State of New York: and these deponents further say, that they personally knew Solomon Parkins, late of Matagorda county, in the State of Texas, and now deceased. And they further say, that the said James, Sarah, and Rufus, and the said Solomon, dec'd, are the legitimate children of Simpson Parkins and Sarah his wife, both late of Montgomery county, State of New York, and now deceased. And the witnesses further depose, that said Solomon Parkins was never married, so far as they have been informed, by general report, and believe; and that the aforesaid James Parkins, Rufus Parkins, and Sarah Tilton, are the next of kin, and immediate and only heirs of so near a degree of consanguinity to the said Solomon Parkins, deceased, and that he had no other brothers or sisters, or their descendants.

"And deponents further say, that they have no direct or indirect interest or claim in the estate of said decedent last-named, and that they are wholly disinterested in the matters herein, and make these depositions without bias, or hope of pecuniary gain.

"SAMUEL SLYKE,
"JONATHAN BARLOW."

"STATE OF NEW YORK, SS. }
Madison County. }

"I, Timothy Bundick, Judge of the Court of ——, the same being a court of record, and having a seal of office, do hereby certify that the foregoing affidavit was made, subscribed, and sworn to before me, by the witnesses, Samuel Slyke and Jonathan Barlow; and I further certify, that I know them to be persons of good standing, and entitled to full credibility.

"In testimony of all which, I have hereunto set my hand, and caused to be impressed thereon the seal of said court, at ——, this —— day of ——, A. D. 1857.

"TIMOTHY BUNDICK,

[L. S.] "*Judge of* ——."

The foregoing proof may also be made before a commissioner for the State of Texas, resident in the State of New York, or any State where the claimants may reside, after the same form. The commissioner is not required by law to use an official seal.

When done before a judge, it is better, for more certainty, to have a certificate from the Secretary of State attached thereto, as follows, viz.:

Form.

"I, Elias W. Leavenworth, Secretary of State for the State of New York, do hereby certify that the Honorable Timothy Bundick, whose name and official seal appears to the foregoing documents, was, on the day of ——, A. D. 18—, Judge of ——, the same being a court of record, with a seal of office, and that full faith and credence are due to all his acts, in that capacity.

"In testimony of all the foregoing, I have hereunto set my hand, and caused to be impressed the great seal of the State of New York. Done at Albany, this —— day of ——, A. D. 18—."

[GREAT SEAL.]

Advice to Heirs.

There are heirs to persons who have died in Texas scattered throughout the United States, Great Britain, and Germany, who have no knowledge of their rights here, or, if they have, too slightly to appreciate them. These inheritances generally consist of land and land claims, and some of them are large and valuable.

The rapid course of time, and railroad speed of events, are constantly attenuating and obliterating the evidences of those rights, and fortifying the titles of adverse claimants. It behoves all such heirs, therefore, who have knowledge of their claims, to be up and doing; for soon "the night cometh, when no man can work:" too soon, the very last vestiges of their rights will be forever beyond all power of resuscitation.

The proper and most expeditious way, is for the *claimant* to entrust his business with a reliable agent — one who has experience, and is familiar with the routine of our laws. Such a person will effect more, in a short time, than the claimant could, unaided, in a whole lifetime.

The land claims of many persons who were soldiers in Texas during the Revolution, and who died in the service, have been tampered with by unauthorized administrations, and sold; but the greater part of such transactions are nullities, and the property may be reclaimed. Many lands, which were owned by persons since deceased, have been sold for State and county taxes; but such can be recovered by the heirs, unless the adverse claimant have actually occupied the land for a sufficient length of time to claim by *proscription.*

Where a person has ever been entitled to any property in Texas, by right of heirship, he or she had better look to such rights, without delay, as the time is fast approaching when the smallest government grant of land will be of far more consideration than at present.

CHAPTER XI.

CONVEYANCES OF REAL ESTATE.

Deeds of conveyance for real estate must be in writing, signed, sealed, and delivered by the *grantor*, and acknowledged by him before a proper officer, for authentication; or acknowledged by him before two witnesses, who, at his request, must sign their names at the bottom, on the left hand side: scroll seals may be used, when recognised in the body of the instrument.

It is said that, where the witnesses are present, and see the grantor sign and execute the instrument, and sign, as witnesses, at the same time, in presence of the grantor, that it is not necessary for the witnessing to be at his request; but, when they sign at a subsequent period, then they must become witnesses, at his (particular) request (see Tex. Rep. vol. xv.) Although the title to slaves passes from the seller to the purchaser by delivery alone, it is better, in order to prevent all subsequent embarrassments, that a written title should be taken, authenticated and recorded according to law. All conveyances for land *certificates*, land *warrants*, and land *scrip*, must be formally executed, like deeds to real estate; but no recording is requisite. A land certificate is not purely real estate, but an *incorporeal hereditament*.

Form of deed in Fee Simple (warrantee).

"THE STATE OF TEXAS,
County of Matagorda. }

"Know all men by these presents, that I, A. B., of the State and county aforesaid, in consideration of the sum of five hundred dollars, to me paid by C. D., of the county of Navarro, State aforesaid, have granted, bargained, sold, released, and conveyed, and by these presents do hereby grant, bargain, sell, release, and convey, unto the said C. D., his heirs or assigns, all that (here describe the premises), together with all and singular the rights, members, hereditaments, and appurtenances to the same belonging, or in any wise incident or appertaining.

"To have and to hold all and singular the premises herein described, unto him, the said C. D., his heirs or assigns forever. And I, the said A. B., do, for myself, my heirs and representatives, hereby warrant, and I will and they shall forever defend, the title to said premises and appurtenances, unto him, the said C. D., his heirs or assigns, against all persons legally claiming the same, or any part thereof. In testimony of all which, I have hereunto set my hand and scroll seal, at Matagorda, this twenty-seventh day of May, A. D. one thousand eight hundred and fifty-seven.

"(Signed) A. B. [SCROLL.]

"Signed, sealed, and delivered in presence of witnesses,

"L. O., P. S."

Remarks.

Covenants can be inserted according to agreement of the parties.

Persons executing instruments in other States, concerning real estate situate in Texas, must recollect that all such instruments must be in conformity with our laws, without any regard to the laws of the place of execution.

Form of authenticating a deed for record, when acknowledged by grantor to the officer.

"THE STATE OF TEXAS,
County of Matagorda. }

"Before me [*Notary Public, County Clerk, or Chief Justice County Court*] personally appeared A. B., to me personally well known, and who acknowledged to me, that he executed and delivered the foregoing instrument of writing in favor of C. D., dated the 27th day of May, A. D. 1857, for the purposes and consideration therein stated; and the said A. B. further acknowledged to me his signature and seal to said instrument of writing, and requested me to authenticate the same.

"To certify all of the foregoing, I have hereunto set my hand and affixed the impress of my seal of office, at Matagorda, this 27th day of May, A. D. 1857.

"LEMUEL SHACKELFORD,

[L. S.] "[*Title of office*]."

Proof of an instrument by a subscribing witness, where he was present at the execution thereof.

"THE STATE OF TEXAS,
County of Matagorda. }

"Before me [any of the foregoing officers] personally appeared L. O., to me personally well known, and who, being by me first duly sworn, according to law, states, on oath, that he saw A. B., grantor in the foregoing instrument of writing, dated May 27th, A. D. 1857, subscribe the same.

"And deponent further says, that he signed the same as a subscribing witness at that time.

"To certify all of which, I have hereunto set my hand and the impress of my seal of office, at Matagorda, this 27th day of May, A. D. 1857.

"PETER JONES,

[L. S.] "[*Official designation*]."

Where the deed is witnessed at a subsequent period from its execution.

"THE STATE OF TEXAS,
County of Matagorda. }

"Before me [any of the foregoing officers] personally appeared L. O., to me personally well known, and who, being by me first duly sworn, according to law, says, on oath, that he signed the foregoing instrument of writing, dated May 27th, 1857, as a subscribing witness, and that he did so at the request of A. B., the grantor therein."

[Same conclusions as foregoing.]

When the subscribing witnesses are dead, or their place of residence is unknown, or when they reside out of the State.

"THE STATE OF TEXAS,
County of Matagorda. }

"Before me [any of the foregoing officers] person ally appeared John Jones, to me personally well known, who, first being duly sworn by me, according to law, deposeth and saith, that L. O. and P. S., whose names appear signed as subscribing witnesses to the foregoing instrument of writing, executed by A. B., and dated May 27th, 1857, [*are non-residents of the State of Texas, or their place of residence is unknown, or they are dead, as the fact may be*].

"(Signed) JOHN JONES.

"Sworn to and subscribed before me, this —— day of ————, A. D. 18—, which I certify, under my hand and seal of office."

[Name, official designation, and seal of office.]

After which the instrument may be proven for record.

"THE STATE OF TEXAS,
County of Matagorda. }

"Before me [any of the foregoing officers] personally appeared John Jones and Samuel Geddes, to me personally well known, who, being by me first duly sworn, according to law, depose and say, that they are well acquainted with the handwriting of A. B. and L. O., the former the grantor, and the latter one of the subscribing witnesses in the foregoing and annexed instrument of writing, dated May 27th, A. D. 1857; and these deponents further say, that said signatures are the true and genuine signatures of said persons, and that they, these deponents, are wholly uninterested in any matters contained in said instrument of writing.

"JOHN JONES,
"SAMUEL GEDDES.

"Subscribed and sworn to before me, this —— day of ————, A. D. 1857, which I hereby certify, under my hand and seal of office."

[Official signature and seal.]

Mode of proof when the subscribing witnesses are personally unknown to the officer.

"THE STATE OF TEXAS,
Matagorda County.

"Before me [any of the foregoing officers] personally appeared Samuel Holliday and Henry Watkins, to me well known, who, being by me first duly sworn, depose and say, that L. O., who now also appears personally present, is the identical person whose name appears signed as one of the subscribing witnesses to the foregoing and annexed instrument of writing, bearing date May 27th, 1857, and executed by A. B.

"SAMUEL HOLLIDAY,
"HENRY WATKINS.

"Subscribed and sworn to before me, this —— day of ————, A. D. 1857, which I hereby certify, under my hand and seal of office."

[Official signature and seal.]

After which the instrument of writing may be proven up by the unknown witness.

"THE STATE OF TEXAS,
County of Matagorda.

"Before me [any of the foregoing officers] personally appeared L. O., a subscribing witness to the annexed instrument of writing, dated May 27th, A. D. 1857, and executed by A. B.: And the identity of the said L. O. having been satisfactorily proven to me by the affidavits of Samuel Holliday and Henry Watkins: And he, the said L. O., having been by me first duly sworn, according to law, now states, on oath, that he saw A. B., the grantor in said instrument of writing, subscribe his name to the same as it there appears. And deponent further says, that he signed his name, as a subscribing witness, to said instrument of writing.

"To certify all which, I have hereto set my hand and affixed the impress of my official seal.

[L. S.] "Done at Matagorda, this —— day of ——, A. D. 1857."

Mode of authenticating an instrument executed by a married woman, concerning her separate property.

In making a conveyance of separate property, or in the execution of any other written instrument, a married woman *must* always be joined therein by her husband. Such instruments can never be proven up by witnesses, but must be authenticated by a Judge of the Supreme or District Court, Notary Public, or Chief Justice of the county.

Form.

"THE STATE OF TEXAS,
County of Matagorda. }

"Before me, Matthew Talbot, Chief Justice of the County Court, in and for said County of Matagorda, personally appeared Elizabeth Hunter, wife of John L. Hunter, both to me personally well known, parties to a certain instrument of writing, bearing date the 21st day of March, A. D. 1857, and hereto annexed; and having been examined by me privily and apart from her said husband, and after having the same read over and fully explained to her by me, she, the said Elizabeth Hunter, acknowledged the same to be her act and deed, and declared that she had willingly and understandingly signed, sealed, and delivered the same, for the purposes and consideration therein expressed, and that she did not wish to retract it. And afterwards, on the same day, personally appeared the abovenamed John L. Hunter, who stated to me, that he had executed said instrument of writing for the purposes and consideration therein expressed, and he acknowledged his signature and seal to the same.

"To certify all of which, I have hereunto set my hand, and caused to be affixed the impress of the seal of said County Court.

"Done at Matagorda, this 29th day of March, A. D. 1857.

"MATTHEW TALBOT,
[L. S.] "*Chief Justice of Matagorda County.*"

An instrument to be used in Texas, when authenticated in any other State or Territory, must be done by a Judge of a Court of Record, having a seal of office, or by a Commissioner for this State.

When in a foreign country, it must be done by some Public Minister, Chargé d'Affaires, or Consul of the United States; and, in all cases, the certificate of the acknowledgment or proof must be attested under the official seal of the officer taking the same.

CHAPTER XII.

LEGAL RIGHTS AND REMEDIES.

Mortgages.

THE practice of taking *mortgages* on real estate, negroes, and personal property, as collateral security for money due on notes, bonds, and accounts, is quite common in this State. Although there is a little ambiguity in the 2d section of the law (Hartley's Digest) concerning foreclosing mortgages on personal property, the District Court is the only tribunal where mortgages on real estate and slaves can be foreclosed.

1. In foreclosing a mortgage, suit may be brought in the county where the mortgaged property is situate, or in the county of defendant's domicil.

2. Where the *mortgagor* is dead, the *mortgagee* or owner of the security, or his agent, must present it to the administrator or executor for acceptance, like all other claims against estates of deceased persons.

3. A note, bond, or other debt, secured by a mortgage, is subject to the laws of limitation, in the same manner as though no mortgage existed.

4. Mortgages may be assigned, and the assignee

becomes entitled to all the rights of the original holder.

5. All mortgages on real estate must be recorded in the county where the property lies, within ninety days from the date of the execution thereof; and mortgages on personal property in the county where the mortgagor lives, within a like period; but a failure to comply with this rule does not forfeit the lien as between the parties to the mortgage.

A prudent regard for security would seem to dictate to the holder of a mortgage to prove it up, and cause it to be recorded without delay, as rights of third persons may injuriously intervene.

I have endeavored, by the following simple forms, to exemplify this kind of security in its different phases, so that any person may comprehend, and be enabled to avail him or herself of it, in business transactions.

"*Matagorda, Texas, May* 1*st*, 1857.

"$15,000·00.

"Twelve months after date, for value received, I promise to pay to C. D., or order, the sum of fifteen thousand dollars, with interest thereon from date, at the rate of ten per cent. per annum.

"(Signed) A. B."

"THE STATE OF TEXAS,
County of Matagorda.

"Know all men, by these presents, that I, A. B., of the State and county aforesaid, for and in consideration of the sum of fifteen thousand dollars, with the interest due and to be due thereon, which sum of money I am indebted to C. D., of the same place, and which indebtedness is more fully evidenced by my promissory note, to him delivered, and copied below (here copy evidence of debt), have, better to secure the payment of my said debt, granted, bargained, sold, alienated, and conveyed, and do, by these presents, hereby grant, bargain, sell, and convey unto the said C. D., his heirs or assigns, forever, all of the following described property, viz. (here describe the property): To have and to hold the same, together with all the rights, members, and hereditaments to the same in any wise incident or appertaining, to him, the said C. D., his heirs or assigns, forever.

"And I, the said A. B., for myself and my heirs, hereby covenant with the said C. D., that I am lawfully seized in fee simple of the herein granted premises, and that they are free from all incumbrances: Provided, always, that this conveyance is made upon this condition, that, if I, the said A. B., shall pay, or cause to be paid, to the said C. D., his heirs or assigns, the full sum of fifteen thousand dollars, as mentioned in said promissory note, on or before the first day of May, A. D. 1858, together with the interest then due thereon, then this instrument to become null and void; otherwise to remain in full force and virtue, and become subject to foreclosure, according to law.

"In testimony of all which, I have hereunto set

my hand and scroll seal, at Matagorda, this first day of June, A. D. one thousand eight hundred and fifty-seven.

"(Signed) A. B. [SCROLL.]

"Signed, sealed, and delivered in presence of witnesses."

Or this form of Mortgages.

Hemphill C. J. in T. R. vol. vi. page 13, remarks as follows: "And here I would suggest the re-adoption of the Spanish, or a more simple form of mortgage. The form in use is deceptive and fictitious. It purports to be a perfect deed of conveyance, with conditions."

"THE STATE OF TEXAS,
County of Matagorda.

"Whereas I, A. B., of the State and county aforesaid, being justly indebted to C. D., of the same place, upon a promissory note, a copy of which is copied below (copy of note). Now, in order better to secure the prompt payment of said recited promissory note, together with the interest thereon, I do hereby mortgage, make over, and convey, unto the said C. D., all of the following described land and premises, viz. (here describe property).

"To have and to hold all of the herein described property, together with all the rights thereto incident or belonging, for the sole purpose of securing the payment of said promissory note, and interest, by foreclosure of this mortgage, if I should make default in the prompt payment thereof.

"In testimony of all which, I have hereunto set my hand and scroll seal, at Matagorda, this first day of June, A. D. one thousand eight hundred and fifty-seven.

"(Signed) A. B. [SCROLL.]

"Signed, sealed, and delivered in presence of witnesses."

Mortgage on Personal Property.

Cotton and sugar-planters frequently desire to obtain money, as *advancements*, from their merchants and factors abroad; and the business is so arranged, that benefits are derived by both parties: the planter gets his accommodation, in the way of a loan, and the factor not only secures himself for the repayment of his money, and interest, but also the profits of selling the planter's sugar and cotton.

Form.

"THE STATE OF TEXAS,
County of Matagorda.

"Whereas I, Samuel Kingston, of the State and county aforesaid, planter, have this day entered into an arrangement and contract with Nelson Clements and Thomas Hayden, commission merchants, doing business in the city and State of New York, under the style of Clements & Hayden, whereby I am to have a credit at their establishment, in said city, up to the amount of four thousand dollars, and I am, from this date, to be allowed to draw drafts on said firm, during the present year, in sums to suit my convenience, until the whole of said sum of money shall have been drawn, or any less amount that I may choose; which drafts they have agreed to promptly honor and pay, according to their tenor. And I, the said Samuel Kingston, in consideration of the foregoing, hereby bind myself and my heirs, to ship or cause to be shipped, in good order, on or before the first day of January next, to the said Clements and Hayden, all of the crop of cotton growing and to be grown on my plantation during the present year; which I estimate will be two hundred bales, of five hundred pounds each. And the said Clements & Hayden are to sell said cotton, on my account, to the best advantage, according to their judgment; and, after deducting the amount of money they may have advanced, and ten per cent. per annum interest thereon, and the other usual charges, to pay the remainder of the proceeds over to me, or my order.

"Now, in order better to secure the repayment of such advances, interest, and charges, in the manner which I have agreed, and as additional security, I do hereby mortgage, pledge, and convey, unto the said Clements & Hayden, all of the following named negro slaves, viz. (here describe the slaves). To have and to hold all of said slaves, together with their increase, for the sole purpose of securing the prompt repayment of said advances of money, be the same more or less, with the interest and charges, in the manner as I have herein contracted.

"But I am to remain in possession of said slaves, and keep them on my plantation, in this county, until a default is made by me, and a foreclosure hereof is decreed, according to law.

"In testimony of all which, I have hereunto set my hand, and seal of office, at Matagorda, this twenty-first day of June, A. D. one thousand eight hundred and fifty-seven.

"SAMUEL KINGSTON. [SCROLL.]

"Signed, sealed, and delivered in presence of witnesses."

The foregoing mortgage, after being properly authenticated, should be filed for record in the county where the mortgagor lives.

Delays are dangerous; and a person who is cautious enough to secure his interest, by taking full security, should certainly not leave the most important part unaccomplished.

Releases of Mortgages.

When a mortgage is paid and satisfied, a release should be procured, to be executed by the mortgagee or assignee of the mortgage security, and the same should be authenticated and recorded, like all other formal instruments.

"THE STATE OF TEXAS, }
County of Matagorda. }

"I, C. D., of the State and county aforesaid, do hereby certify and acknowledge, that a deed of mortgage, bearing date the —— day of ——, A. D. 1856, and recorded in the county record-book G, page 350, of the proper records of said county, and including the following property (here describe the property), and executed by A. B., to me, the said C. D., for better securing the payment of his promissory note for six thousand dollars, dated on the first day of January, A. D. 1856, payable one year after date, with interest, at the rate of ten per cent. per annum, from date, has this day been fully paid and satisfied; and, therefore, every matter, thing, and security contained in said mortgage, is hereby fully released, and the property described therein, together with all its rights, is hereby reconveyed to the said A. B., free from all incumbrances on account of said debt.

"In testimony of all which, I have hereunto set my hand, and scroll seal, at Matagorda, this third day of January, A. D. one thousand eight hundred and fifty-seven.

"(Signed) C. D. [SCROLL.]

"Signed, sealed, and delivered in presence of witnesses."

Liens.

According to various decisions of our Supreme Court, an equitable lien exists, in favor of the vendor,

against the specific property in the hands of the vendee, and subsequent purchasers, with notice.

Statute Liens.

All judgments of courts of record are liens on all real estate in the county of the *forum*, provided executions are properly issued.

Builders and mechanics have liens, in the nature of mortgages, on all buildings which they erect or work on, and on the ground on which such buildings are erected or worked on, until compensation is made to them for such, and for the materials furnished. In order to secure this lien, a contract must be made, in writing, and recorded within thirty days.

Every person who furnishes supplies, or does repairs or labor, for any domestic vessel, has a lien on such vessel and her freight money, for the security and payment of the same.

Married Women.

When the homestead is sold, it is necessary for the wife to join in the conveyance, and it must be authenticated in this State, by a Judge of the Supreme or District Court, Chief Justice, Notary Public, or County Clerk.

The law requires every married woman to make out a schedule of all her separate property, and present the same to the County Clerk, and acknowledge it for record.

Schedule.

"THE STATE OF TEXAS,
County of Matagorda.

"Be it known to all persons whom it may concern, that I, Julia Dean, wife of Thomas Dean, all of the State and county aforesaid, being the true and lawful owner of the following property, in my own separate right, do make this, my schedule, for the purposes of record, viz. (here describe property). The same was acquired by me by inheritance from my father, Jarvis Subtlet, deceased, late of Munroe County, Alabama.

"And I have made this schedule of all the property which I own in my separate right, for the purpose of having it recorded, according to law.

"In testimony of all which, I have hereto signed my name, in Matagorda, this first day of July, A. D. one thousand eight hundred and fifty-seven.

"JULIA DEAN."

"THE STATE OF TEXAS,
County of Matagorda.

"Before me, James H. Selkirk, Clerk of the County Court for the county aforesaid, personally appeared Julia Dean, wife of Thomas Dean, all of the State and county aforesaid, and presented to me the foregoing schedule of her separate property for registration, and she acknowledged said instrument to be her act and deed, for the purposes therein expressed.

[L. S.] "To certify all which, I have hereunto set my hand and seal of office, at Matagorda, this second day of June, A. D. 1857."

Remarks and Advice.

It is always advisable for married women, in this State, and more particularly if strangers, when they first emigrate to it, if they own property in their own right, to designate, and cause it to be recorded in the proper county. Husbands, like all other human beings, are fallible, and liable not only to errors, but to all the vicissitudes of fickle fortune; and the wife's ample property too often is made a sacrifice to her own negligence in not giving publicity to her separate rights. The expense and trouble are very little, and the security which it affords more than repays. And it is also a duty, which the husband not only owes to his wife and family, but to the public, to attend to this matter, so that he may appear before the world in his true character and circumstances; not apparently wealthy in property, which really belongs to his wife, and himself, perhaps, insolvent. The laws of our State have persistently endeavored to protect and guard the rights of married women; but if they will, in despite of such care, keep silent, and allow husbands to improvidently control their separate property, disastrous law-suits, and even total sacrifice, may follow. Therefore, I say to you, let it be properly made public what your separate rights are, and there is little danger that they will ever be contested; and, if they unfortunately should, the laws and juries of this State will see your rights protected.

The property rights of married persons emigrating to this State are governed by the laws of their marriage domicil. It is true, the existence of the woman, by marriage, becomes merged in that of her husband, and her rights subject to his control, for better or for worse, but the wisdom of our law-makers has provided means by which the wife may not only fulfil all the behests of her high station, be a dutiful and affectionate companion, and still save for herself and her progeny her own separate property, without doing violence to her proper affections and confidence. In fact, all the servile *wife*-slavery of the old common law has been abrogated here, and a just medium been established between the severity of that and the license of the civil law. By our system the conjugal relations are preserved, and the legal restraints are very wholesome checks against improvident, reckless, and wicked practices of bad husbands.

All property purchased during coverture, with proceeds of the community, or with the joint or separate earnings of husband or wife, even if the conveyance be made directly to the wife, inures to the community.

A married woman can, by last will and testament, dispose of her separate and her community rights.

Limitation Laws.

1. All suits on open accounts, excepting between merchant and merchant, must be brought within *two* years. Each item in an open account is the *data* by which to compute the time.

2. Suits on notes, and other written obligations for money, must be commenced within *four* years after the same became due.

3. Persons absent *seven* years from the estate without being heard from, are presumed to be dead.

4. When a claim of any kind is once barred by the law of limitation, it cannot be revived or taken out of the operation of the law, excepting by an acknowledgment in writing, signed by the person to be charged thereby.

5. Five years of peaceable possession of land under color of title, with deed duly proven and recorded, bars all other claims, except of *minors, femes covert,* and persons *non compos.*

6. Peaceable possession of land under a defective title, emanating from the sovereignty of the soil, is a bar, in *three* years, to adverse claimants.

7. Any person holding peaceable possession of real estate *five* years, cultivating or using the same, and paying tax thereon, under a deed duly recorded, secures a good title, precluding *all* others.

8. Ten years' peaceable possession, and cultivation or use of 640 acres of land, gives the holder a perfect title.

9. All contracts concerning lands and slaves, if not to be performed within one year, must be reduced tc writing, and signed by the party to be charged therewith, or by his lawful agent, otherwise the same is within the *statute of frauds.*

10. All fraudulent conveyances, made for the purpose of secreting the debtor's property from his creditors, are deed-void in law.

11. When any pretended loan of goods or slaves is made to any person, and that person remains in possession *three years*, without demand made on the part of the pretended lender, then such property becomes liable for the debts of the borrower.

12. The adverse possession of a slave, for the term of two years, bars the rightful owner's title and claim.

13. When any person dies against whom there is cause of action, the statute of limitations ceases to run until twelve months after such death, unless an administrator or executor be qualified before that time.

14. In case of the death of any person in whose favor there is a cause of action, the statute ceases to run, under like circumstances as above.[1]

Supreme Court.

Civil suits are taken from the District Courts to the Supreme Court by *appeal* or *writ of error;* the former

[1] The filing of a petition in the District Court, on any claim, and the issuance of process from Justice's Court, are the dates at which the limitation stops running; that is, if the claim was not barred then, it will be secured from prescription by such acts.

must be moved for at the term of the court at which the cause is tried, but the latter may be prosecuted at any time within two years. The jurisdiction of this court is appellate, excepting the power to grant certain remedial writs.

It is composed of one Chief Justice and two Associate Justices.

The terms of the court are as follows:

At Austin, third Mondays in October, and continue *nine* weeks, or until business is finished.

At Galveston, first Mondays in January, and continue *ten* weeks.

At Tyler, first Mondays in April, and may continue until *first of July*.

District Courts — Collection of Debts, and Remedies.

There are eighteen judicial districts in the State, and the judge of each district holds two sessions of court in each county in his district every year. The District Courts have original jurisdiction of all suits, complaints, and pleas whatever, without any distinction between law and equity, when the matter in controversy shall be of the value of, or amount to, one hundred dollars, exclusive of interest.

Causes decided in the justices' courts may be removed to this court for trial *de novo*, within ninety days, by *certiorari*, on the party applying showing, by an affidavit, sufficient cause to the judge. There is no direct appeal from justices' courts.

Proceedings in the County Courts pertaining to the

estates of deceased persons and wards, may be removed to the district courts for revision, at any time within two years, by certiorari.

The district courts are the tribunals where all suits for debts of over hundred dollars are brought: the district and justices' courts have concurrent jurisdiction, when the amount is just one hundred dollars.

On a promissory note, judgment is usually rendered at the first term of court, after due service of the writ, unless the service were made by publication, when two terms of court are required to obtain a judgment.

Judgments on promissory notes bear interest according to the rate stipulated therein—not to exceed twelve per cent.

Immediately after the rising of court, executions are required by law to be issued on all judgments of the term, and placed in the hands of the sheriff. If the first execution is not satisfied, a new one should be issued every six months, or after every term of court. Judgments, in this court, are liens on all the real estate in the county, provided executions are properly issued. Personal property must be levied on before lien attaches: to constitute a good levy on the same, actual possession must be taken by the sheriff. All property sold by execution is without any appraisement. Sales, by execution, of real estate and negroes, are made on the first Tuesday of every month, after twenty days' notice, by written advertisements. Personal property can be sold at any time, after ten days' notice.

This court is empowered to issue the summary writs of attachment and garnishment. The proceeding is as follows: The plaintiff files, in the office of the clerk of this court, his petition against the defendant, setting forth his cause, in the ordinary form; and if, at any time after such filing, he desires a writ of *attachment*, and can make affidavit, in due form, it will be issued. The causes for granting an attachment are: 1. That the defendant is justly indebted to the plaintiff, and the amount of the demand, and that the defendant is not a resident of this State; 2. Or, that he is about to remove out of this State; 3. Or, that he secretes himself, so that the ordinary process of law cannot be served on him; 4. Or, that he is about to remove his property beyond this State, and that thereby the plaintiff will probably lose his debt; 5. Or, that he is about to remove his property beyond the county; 6. Or, that he is about to transfer or secrete, or has transferred or secreted, his property, for the purpose of defrauding his creditors, and thereby the plaintiff will probably lose his debt.

The plaintiff must also, in addition to any of these propositions, swear that the attachment is not sued out for the purpose of injuring the defendant.

Affidavit.

"THE STATE OF TEXAS, } *In District Court.*
County of Matagorda. }

"Before me, R. L., Clerk of the District Court for the county aforesaid, personally appeared G. T., the plaintiff in a suit now pending in said District Court, entitled 'No. — G. T. *vs.* A. B.,' who, after being by me duly sworn, according to law, deposes and says, that the said A. B. is justly indebted to him, the deponent, in the sum of (here describe the debt). Affiant further says, that the said A. B. is not a resident of this State (or any of the other causes), and that thereby the plaintiff will probably lose his debt. Affiant also swears, that this attachment is not sued out for the purpose of injuring the defendant.

"(Signed) G. T.

"Subscribed and sworn to before me, this first day of May, A. D. 1857, which I hereby certify under my my hand and seal of office.

"R. L.—*Clerk D. C. M. C.*"

This affidavit may be made by an agent or attorney for the plaintiff. A bond is required to be filed with the affidavit, in double the amount sworn to be due.

The plaintiff may, at any time after filing his petition, affidavit and bond, or, at the same time, obtain writs of attachment against defendant's property, and writs of garnishment against any persons supposed to be indebted to the defendant, or supposed to have any of the defendant's effects or property.

The foregoing summary proceedings, it will be recollected, are all before judgment; and, if said proceedings are improvidently had, the defendant may, on the trial, plead damages, in reconvention or set-off.

In ordinary suits for debt or damages, after the plaintiff has obtained a judgment, and no property can be found whereon to levy an execution, the plaintiff, his agent, or attorney, may have a *writ* of garnishment, by applying to the clerk of the court from which the execution issued, and making an affidavit.

Writ of Attachment.

"THE STATE OF TEXAS TO THE SHERIFF OF MATAGORDA COUNTY, GREETING:

"We command you, that you attach so much of the property of A. B., if to be found in your county, repleviable on security, as shall be of value sufficient to make the sum of (here insert amount claimed), together with the legal interest thereon, from the —— day of ——, A. D. 1857, and costs, to satisfy the demand of G. T., and such property, so attached, in your hands to keep and secure, that the same may be liable to further proceedings, thereupon to be had at our next District Court, to be holden in the court-house, in the city of Matagorda, within and for said county of Matagorda, on the second Monday after the first Monday in October next, so as to compel the said A. B. to appear and plead to the complaint of the said G. T., when and where you shall make known how you have executed this writ.

"*Attest.*—R. L., Clerk of said District Court. Given under my hand and the seal of said court, at Matagorda, this —— day of ——, A. D. 18—.

[L. S.] "R. L.—*Clerk D. C. M. C.*"

The legal mode of levying an attachment on personal property, is by the officer going to the place where the property is, and then and there declaring, in the presence of one or more credible persons of the neighborhood, that he attaches said property as the property of defendant.

Writ of Garnishment.

"THE STATE OF TEXAS TO THE SHERIFF OF MATAGORDA COUNTY, GREETING:

"Whereas, G. T., plaintiff, has filed, in the District Court of Matagorda county, State of Texas, his petition, bond, and affidavit, in a suit against A. B., defendant, and obtained from said court an original attachment against the property of him, said A. B., and the said plaintiff having applied to me for a writ of garnishment against one C. M., a resident of said county:

"These are, therefore, to command you that you summon the said C. M., as garnishee in this case, to be and appear, on the first day of the first term of our said District Court, to be holden at the court-house, in the city of Matagorda, within and for said county of Matagorda, on the second Monday after the first Monday in October next, then and there to answer, upon oath, what he, the said C. M., is indebted to said defendant, or what effects of the defendant he has in his possession, and had at the time of serving this writ of garnishment, and what credits and effects there are of the defendant in the hands of any other person, and what person, to the best of his knowledge and belief.

"And you are commanded to make return of this writ according to the tenor hereof, certifying how you have executed the same.

"Attest: R. L.—*Clerk of said District Court.*

"Given under my hand and seal of office, at Matagorda, this —— day of ————, A. D. 1857.

[L. S.] "R. L.—*Clerk D. C. M. C.*"

The form of a writ of garnishment issued after judgment, is somewhat variant.

Writs of Sequestration

May be issued by judges and clerks of the district courts, and justices of the peace, in the following cases:

1. Where a married woman sues for divorce, and makes oath that she fears her husband will waste her separate property, or their community property, or remove the same, during the pendency of the suit, out of this State, &c.

2. When a person sues for the title or possession

of a slave, or other movable property or chattels, and makes oath that he fears the defendant, or person in possession, will injure or ill-treat such slave, or waste such property, or remove the same out of the State during the pendency of the suit.

3. When a person sues for the foreclosure of a mortgage, or the enforcement of a lien upon a slave, or movable property of any description, and makes oath that he fears the defendant, or person in possession, will injure or ill-treat such slave, or waste such property, or remove such property or slave out of the county.

4. When any person sues for the title or possession of real estate, and makes oath that he fears the defendant, or person in possession, may make use of his possession to injure such property, or waste the fruits and revenue produced by the same, or convert them to his own use.

5. When any person sues for the title or possession of any property from which he has been ejected by force or violence, and makes oath to the facts.

The person applying for a writ of sequestration, must, in all cases, first make affidavit of sufficient facts, and file that, together with his bond, in the Court in which his suit is pending. The bond is made payable to the defendant for a sum of money equal to double the value of the property to be sequestrated.

These proceedings can be had only after petition filed in court.

Form of Sequestration.

"THE STATE OF TEXAS TO THE SHERIFF OF MATAGORDA COUNTY, GREETING:

"You are hereby commanded to take into your possession the following described property, if to be found in your county, to wit (here describe the property), and it safely keep, subject to the future order of our said District Court, unless J. P., who is defendant herein, or any other person, in whose possession all or any of the aforesaid property shall be held, shall replevy the same, according to law.

"Herein fail not, and make due return of this writ to the office of the Clerk of the District Court for said county of Matagorda, on or before the second Monday after the first Monday in October next.

"Attest: R. L.,

"*Clerk of said District Court.*

[L. S.] "Given under my hand and seal of office," &c.

Property exempt from Forced Sale.

By the law of 1839, there was reserved to *every* citizen *or* head of a family, free from execution, fifty acres of land, or one town lot, including his or her homestead and improvements, not exceeding five hundred dollars in value; all household and kitchen furniture, not to exceed two hundred dollars in value; all implements of husbandry, not to exceed fifty dollars in value; all tools, apparatus, and books belonging to the trade or profession of any citizen; five milch-cows (and calves), one yoke of work oxen or one horse (mule), twenty hogs, and one year's provision.

The Constitution of the State of Texas, adopted in 1846, altered that portion of the above exemption which relates to homesteads, but allowed the other portions of the old law to remain for future action by the Legislature.

By the Constitution, "the homestead of a family, not to exceed two hundred acres of land (not included in a town or city lot), or any town or city lot or lots, in value not to exceed two thousand dollars, is exempt from execution, and reserved to the family. It will be perceived, that by the old law the exemptions applied to every citizen *or* head of a family, and that, by the constitutional provision, the homestead exemption is entirely changed, and only applies to heads of families; the remainder of the old exemption law is still in force, and single men avail themselves of it, while heads of families claim under the Constitution.

By the old law, the valuation of the homestead applies to the land or lot, and all improvements thereon; by the constitutional provision, the valuation seems to relate specifically to the soil. The owner of a homestead, if a married man, cannot alienate it unless by consent of the wife, manifested in the conveyance, as I have before shown. Neither can the homestead be mortgaged for any debt or contract, even if the deed of mortgage be made with all the formalities required in an alienation of same property, for the reason, that the intent and end of a mortgage is judicial foreclosure, and a forced sale.

The only mode by which the homestead of a married man can be made to act the part of a collateral security, is to get the husband and wife to execute a deed of trust on it, with power in the trustee to sell on failure of payment. The homestead rights are not acquired in a piece of property against the person from whom purchased, until the property is paid for. The husband and wife, although ever so much involved in debt, may sell their homestead, and collect the money therefor, free from hinderance on the part of creditors.

Thus, it is seen, that our laws are paternal and equitable, in making wise provisions for the shelter and protection of the wife and helpless family from the ruthless attacks of ever-vigilant creditors, and from the inevitable ruin incident to the conduct of dissipated and profligate husbands. In misfortune, sickness, and old age, the husband and wife, if they have been provident enough, in their prosperity, to secure a home, have one sacred retreat, which the shafts of creditors cannot reach; debts, judgments, and executions, are as paper pellets thrown at a castle wall. Nothing conduces so much to the happiness, patriotism, and independence of a people, and to the permanent prosperity and good order of a State, as judicious homestead laws.

The hearthstone of the family, although its members may be bowed down with sorrow and affliction, and though dire poverty, misfortune, and distress, may have assailed on every side, and even entered at the door, becomes an altar for the stricken family circle, where hope for brighter days is engendered, and parental and filial love soothe the broken spirits; where the holy peace within contrasts strangely with the tempest of misery without. Is not that man more noble, who can utter, with the intense feelings of confident independence — "This domicil, which shelters my family, although humble; this soil, which I till for bread, is theirs and mine; and no power of law, or force of circumstances, can wrest it from us"?

If I had a voice in framing a system of laws, and sincerely desired to imbue the people with honest principles, to make virtue and industrious habits predominate, I would endeavor to exempt from forced sale ample homesteads.

The want of such a protection is a fruitful source, in many countries, of vagabondism, crime, and immorality.

Creditors are too prone to view all *exemption* laws as merely the coverts for rogues and cheats; but, in taking this view of the matter, they are only calculating their own immediate losses or gains.

The inhabitants of a State, who, under adversity, are protected from total ruin by homestead laws, are far more to be relied on in their contracts, as a general thing, than those who have no such safeguard;

and the aggregate of bad debts, broken contracts, and absconding debtors, will be much greater under the rigid rule of *strip a man of all he hath*, than under the latter system.

If a few fraudulent debtors are unjustly shielded under our *good* laws, how many more debtors are there, who, by their effect, are enabled to remain honest, to eventually extricate themselves from pecuniary involvements, and, in the end, to pay their debts?

The debtor who has a permanent domicil, and an interest in the soil, which he can call the property of himself and family beyond all peradventure, however much he is buffeted by adverse fortune, still maintains a sense of moral dignity and self-esteem, that are incentives to retrieve his true position.

The one system would endeavor to make the unfortunate heads of families enemies to all law, and outcasts and lepers of society, while the other fosters and encourages them in well-doing, and makes them supporters of the laws and institutions of their country. One is an enemy of society, the other an *ægis* for the well-being of our fellow-citizens, and a great advance in the happy results of civilization.

Much, in times past, has been written and said in favor of imprisonment for debt, and the same, and no better reasons, may be urged by those relentless Jews, who are in favor of abolishing the last earthly refuge of unfortunate human nature. Let us, then, be thankful, and rejoice that we live under a government of benign institutions, and that the laws are not antagonistic to virtue and happiness. Let it be the first and last solicitude of every head of a family to look well to the future protection of those whom Heaven has entrusted to their care. Every husband should consider it a sacred duty, whether rich or poor, to make preparation according to his means, that the partner of his joys and sorrows, and his little ones, may not, in the event of his early death or ruinous misfortune, be cast upon the cold world, homeless and unsheltered; such a fate, superadded to other troubles, is sufficient to turn aside from the paths of rectitude and morality those tender hearts that before knew no guile. Sickness, misfortune, and death, are common to all men, and poverty is the normal state of all; affluence is not always the result of well-laid plans, and wealth falls only to the lot of a favored few.

The ownership of a homestead imparts to the family an independence and self-reliance which the mere tenant, and his dependent family, can never enjoy; tenancy is a relic of *feudal* times; the condition of the lower orders, in all despotic and over-peopled governments; and no family, in a country like this, should occupy so degraded a position.

County Courts.

Each county has its county court, which consists of a chief justice and clerk, and has jurisdiction in all matters concerning the probating of last wills, granting letters of administration, letters of guardianship and settlement, and supervision of deceased persons' and minors' and lunatics' estates.

The clerk is also recorder of deeds, mortgages, and all other instruments of writing which require to be recorded.

This court holds its sessions on the last Mondays of every month.

All claims, of whatever nature, against deceased persons' estates, must be sworn to by the owner or agent, and presented to the administrator or executor thereof, within twelve months after the grant of administration or executorship, for acceptance. After approval, they must be presented to the chief justice for approval; and, if not presented within twelve months, such claims are postponed until the payment of all those presented within due time.

If a claim be presented, duly authenticated, to an executor or administrator, and he or she rejects it, then the owner of such claim must bring suit in the district or justice's court (according to amount) within three months, or the claim is barred.

When a judgment is rendered against an estate on a money claim, it runs that the same be paid in due course of administration, and no execution can be issued.

Justices' Courts.

Each county is divided into a convenient number of justices' precincts, and two justices are elected for each precinct. They are designated Class No. 1 and Class No. 2. No. 1 holds court on the first Saturday of every month for civil business, and No. 2 on the last Saturday.

All civil suits can be brought in this court where the amount or value does not exceed one hundred dollars, exclusive of interest and costs.

The trials and proceedings in this court are conducted with very little formality, and it is very unusual that any written pleadings are filed. The rules of evidence are the same as in district courts.

This is not a court of record.

Justices of the Peace have jurisdiction as at common law, to *comprehend all vagorem men*, and are general conservators of the peace and good morals.

Promissory Notes.

In a country of such vast extent as Texas, with such varieties of soil, climate, and production, offering so many and such various inducements for trade, speculations and employment, men frequently change their abiding places, and perhaps the person whom you, six months ago, contracted with, in one of the seaboard counties, is now a resident of the most extreme portion of the State, five or six hundred miles distant; and this distance, with our facilities of communication, is as much here as so many thousands of miles in some other regions.

And it frequently becomes very inconvenient for the creditor to follow up his debtor, and be obliged to sue, under great disadvantages, in a remote county from the one of the contract. In order to obviate this, the law has provided that where a person contracts to pay or perform in a particular county, he may be sued in that county, or in the county of his domicil; therefore, in taking a promissory note, or other obligation, it is better to pursue a form that will secure this advantage.

Form.

"MATAGORDA, TEXAS, *July* 1, 1857.

"750·00.

"Twelve months after date, for value received, I promise to pay to Richard Roe, or order, the sum of seven hundred and fifty dollars, with interest, at the rate of ten per cent. per annum, from date, until paid. And I hereby further agree to pay this note in the city and county of Matagorda.

"(Signed) JOHN DOE.'

CHAPTER XIII.

LANDS: HOW THEY ARE ACQUIRED IN TEXAS.

THE State of Texas holds the eminent domain of all the public lands within her limits; and all titles to lands, since the Declaration of Independence, have issued directly from the government.

The United States have no authority over, or right of interference in, our land system; and, so far as that is concerned, we are still an independent nation. The vast extent of our public lands, over and above all liabilities, constitutes a fund which places Texas, in point of wealth, far in advance of all the other States. It is true that this is, at present, dormant capital, but increasing in money value; and can, at any time, by legislative enactment, be called into active use. The land-grants of Texas are divided into two great classes: the first consists of specifically designated lands, granted directly by the sovereignty, or a subordinate authority, to the individual. The second class consists of inchoate rights to lands, evidenced by certificates and scrip, issued from various departments of government, on paper, calling for a certain number of acres; and entitles the holder or owner to locate and appropriate any of the public domain, not otherwise withdrawn. These certificates and scrip are evidences of debt against the government, payable in land when applied for.

The first species comprises all the land titles emanating from Spain, Mexico, and the Empresario grants to colonists, and are all in the Spanish language, under rights accruing previous to March 2, 1836, at which time Texas was declared an independent republic. On Nov. 13, 1835, the land-offices were closed, by the Provisional government, and all land transactions were suspended; but the Empresario contracts were in force until the severance from Mexico; that is, colonists were allowed to be introduced, up to that date, under their supervision.

On Dec. 22, 1836, a general land-office was established, at the seat of government, the chief officer being named commissioner: this officer was empowered to execute all acts touching the public lands, and had the custody of all books and archives concerning the same; and all the documents in possession of the various Empresarios were ordered to be transferred and filed in this office.

The commissioner also became the only source from which government titles or patents could issue, and they were to be countersigned by the President of the Republic.

Texas was also divided into land districts, with a subordinate land-office in each: a surveyor-general was appointed for each district, who had deputies, to perform the public surveying: there was also a register and receiver for each; and any person who was entitled to land could have the same surveyed, by appearing before the register and receiver, and making proof of his or her right: the survey, after being made, is sent to the general land-office, for patent.

Soon after, all the functions of the several land-offices were suspended, by different laws, until the first Thursday in January, 1838; and, by the subsequent act, opening the land-office, the whole system was remodelled, and the very expensive machinery heretofore in use abolished. Up to this time, *no* land certificates had been issued, excepting to soldiers.

The new system established in every county a board of land commissioners, whose duty it was to investigate the rights of applicants for head-right certificates, to take testimony, and to issue or to reject: if rejected, the claimant had the right of appeal to the next term of the District Court for the county. Head-right certificates, issued by these boards, could be located on any of the public domain, provided that persons having head-rights, by emigration, before March 2, 1836, had a right to make selections six months previous to those who emigrated after that time.

All persons entitled to lands, and who had procured surveys to be made, previous to the closing of the general land-office, in 1835, but who had not received titles, were entitled to patents for the same. The head-right certificates, issued by the foregoing local boards, I shall, for convenience, designate as first-class and second-class — the latter of which had *certain conditions* attached.

On January 29, 1840, Congress passed a law, making two boards of travelling land commissioners, consisting of three persons each, who visited every county, and examined the records of the local boards, and took testimony concerning each head-right certificate which had been issued: they then reported to the general land-office, recommending for patents all certificates which they had adjudged good, and rejecting all which could not, or were omitted to be, satisfactorily reproven to them. Many persons, honestly entitled to their certificates, lost them, by the death or absence of the witnesses by whom they first established their rights, before the *local* boards — not having anticipated this readjudication of rights which they deemed fully vested by law.

It is true, the travelling commissioners reported to the general land-office the good and the rejected certificates; but the certificates themselves not being before them, in their investigations, those that were condemned, on their face, appeared, to the uninitiated, as fair as those that were recommended; and hundreds of persons, both in Texas and the United States, were deceived and defrauded, in purchasing them; and many such are still afloat. There is no doubt, that the local boards, being influenced, in some instances, by gain, and, in others, through carelessness, issued many land certificates to persons not entitled, or on very frail proof; but it was far better that the government should suffer, through its agents, than that individuals should be imposed on by the government, acting through persons of its own selection.

Claimants whose head-right certificates had been rejected by the travelling board, had, until July, 1847, a right of appeal to the district courts, or, more properly, of suing the State in said courts; and, by a recent act, they can now bring their cases before the Court of Claims, at Austin.

Under the colonization laws, every head of a family, whose occupation was farming and stock-raising, was entitled to a league and labor (4605 acres); if only stock-raising, one league (4428 acres). Every single man was entitled to one-fourth of a league (1107 acres); but it was very common for two single men to unite, call themselves a family, and obtain a whole league: these latter grants are now considered beyond investigation. The land claims issued by Texas, since she became disconnected from Mexico, are head-right certificates, military certificates, land-scrip, which was sold by agents of the Republic of Texas, various premium certificates, school certificates, public improvement certificates, and colony head-right certificates.

Persons who were living in Texas at the date of the Declaration of Independence (March 2, 1836), were considered citizens; and all citizens living in Texas at the adoption of the Constitution (March 17, 1836), and who had not received their land, were entitled to it, in like manner as the colonists of the Empresarios. Volunteer soldiers, who arrived in Texas between March 2, 1836, and August 1, 1836, and had received honorable discharges from the army, were entitled to head-rights, in the same proportion as the original colonists.

Of Head-rights, First Class.

1. Every head of a family, where the family resided in the country, was entitled to a head-right certificate of one league and labor of land.

2. Every single man, of the age of seventeen years and upwards, was entitled to a head-right certificate of one-third of a league.

3. All persons who had, under any of the colonization laws, received their leagues of land, as heads of families, and their quarter of a league, as single men, were entitled to an additional quantity, viz., enough to increase the league to one league and labor, and the quarter of a league to one-third: this being an additional grant of 177 acres to the married man, and 369 acres to the single man.

4. Single men, who were in Texas on March 2, 1836, and who were entitled, under the Constitution, to one-third of a league of land, became, by marrying, before Dec. 14, 1838, entitled to an augmentation of two-thirds of a league and one labor, or 3128 acres, additional.

5. By a law passed Dec. 18, 1837, all persons who had then been permanently disabled in the military

service of Texas, were each entitled to one league and labor of land (*extra*)—the certificates for which were to be issued by the local boards.

The local boards had no authority to issue any of the foregoing land certificates, after the second Monday in March, 1840.

The head-right certificates of the first class had no subsequent conditions attached.

Of Head-rights, Second Class.

Every single free white man, who was not entitled to a head right of first class, provided he arrived in Texas previous to Oct. 1, 1837, was entitled to a conditional head-right certificate of 640 acres, and every head of a family to a conditional certificate of 1280 acres. The conditions were, that the grantee, and his family, should remain in the country three years, and do and perform all the duties required of other citizens; after which time, the grantee was entitled to an unconditional certificate.

All of the second class of claimants who were single men, and had married before 1st October, 1837, were entitled to an additional certificate of 640 acres, making the same amount as to persons who emigrated with their families.

On the 15th January, 1841, local boards were organized for the purpose of issuing unconditional certificates to all those persons who had received conditional certificates of second and third classes.

By a subsequent amendment, these boards became

empowered to issue unconditional certificates of the second and third classes, to all persons who had become entitled by length of residence, without ever having obtained *conditionals:* the applicant was obliged to make proof as foregoing.

By a law of 1848, the local boards were prohibited from issuing any land certificates, excepting to those persons who had, under previous laws, obtained conditional certificates.

Up to the first day of February, 1856, there were, with certain intervals, local boards of land commissioners in every county, which tribunals were empowered to issue unconditional land certificates (only).

Of Head-Rights — Third Class.

Heads of families, who emigrated to Texas with their families, after October, 1837, and before the 1st day of January, 1840, were entitled to head-rights of 640 acres, and single men to half of the amount.

The conditions for third class were the same as in second class; provided, that no sale of a conditional certificate of the third class was valid.

The act granting third class head-rights speaks of a *conditional* and *unconditional* grant of *land;* does not use the word *certificate;* still the boards of commissioners issued land certificates under the law, in the same form as second class head-rights. I think the Legislature intended that the emigrants should select their quantum of land from the public domain, and procure it to be recognised in some way by the local boards; and, after a residence of three years, that they should be entitled to an unconditional title for the specific land. Unconditional certificates were granted on third class conditional certificates until February 1st, 1856.

Of Head-Rights — Fourth Class.

Heads of families, emigrating with their families after the first of January, 1840, and before the first of January, 1842, were entitled to conditional head-right certificates of 640 acres each, and single men to half the amount. Conditions same as in the foregoing.

Of Military Land Claims.

All persons who performed military services under the Republic of Texas, in any regularly organized company, up to 1838, were entitled to land certificates in the following ratio, over and above their head-rights, viz: For three months' services, 320 acres; for six months, 640 acres; for nine months, 960 acres; for twelve months, or more (in one tour of duty), 1280 acres.

Of Special Military Grants.

1. All soldiers who were in the battle of San Jacinto (April 21st, 1836), were entitled to extra land certificates for 640 acres each, called donation.

2. The soldiers who took part in the reduction of

Bexar (December, 1835), were entitled to land certificates of 640 acres each.

3. Those who were in the action of March, 1836, under the command of Cols. Fannin and Ward, were entitled to land certificates of 640 acres.

4. The heirs of those who fell at the Alamo, under Bowie and Travis, were entitled to like extra amount.

The heirs of the above men who were single, were entitled in all, including head-right, to 4036 acres, and, if married, to 7165 acres. The recipients of donation certificates were at first prohibited from selling or assigning them; but the law has been repealed, and they now stand on the same footing of other certificates.

Soldiers' land certificates, of the various kinds, are a large and truly meritorious class of claims against the public domain, but, by the destruction of the adjutant general's office, in 1855, and the law establishing the court of claims, much distrust and difficulty has been thrown around them, while other kinds, of an inferior grade of merit, have been more favored.

Of Locations and Surveys.

1. A land certificate of any kind may be located in two tracts, and the owner receives two separate patents.

2. District surveyors are allowed $3 for every lineal mile actually run.

3. The State is divided into thirty-six surveyors'

districts, and each district includes several counties, and has a public surveyor.

4. A person having a land certificate, and being desirous to locate it, writes a description of the vacant tract of land that he selects, and hands it, together with his certificate, to the surveyor, whereupon it is surveyed.

5. All locations and surveys must be returned to the General Land Office within twelve months after location, or both certificate and land become forfeited. A certificate once located can never be raised.

6. Agents charge for locating, surveying, procuring patent, and paying all expenses, one-third of the land, or fifteen cents per acre.

CHAPTER XIV.

COURT OF CLAIMS.

On the 1st of August, 1856, our Legislature passed a law establishing a Court of Claims, which is a tribunal of unprecedented and most extensive and *arbitrary* power. *All* land claims come under the scrutiny of the commissioner of this court, and are by him to be examined and re-adjudicated on, excepting head-rights, of the first and second classes, which have been passed on by the travelling boards, and excepting certificates issued to colonists of Peter's, Mercer's, Castro's, and Fisher and Miller's colonies, and the premium certificates of said colonies, and some few other special certificates of *modern* invention.

All persons who were entitled to land claims, under any of the laws granting head-rights or military land certificates, and who never received their rights, may obtain the same by making the like proof before the commissioner, that would have entitled them by the respective laws under which they claim. The claimant must also prove identity. The applicant and witnesses, if claiming in any other way than by heirship, must appear in person before the court at Austin, which makes the business rather unprofitable; the appropriate record evidence must also be made.

All persons holding any kinds of land certificates, excepting first and second class head-rights, and colonists' and special *civil* certificates, must present them to the commissioner of claims, for *examination* and *registration*, within two years from the 1st day of September, 1856, or they will be forever barred from location and patent, and, in fact, become of no value.

All persons having land certificates, or any interest in such property, should bear this in mind; the time, even now, is too short, and many will be severe sufferers by their neglect or want of information.

Even those land certificates that have been located, surveyed, and returned to the General Land Office long since, if they had not been patented on the passage of this law, are subject to all the conditions and restrictions therein contained.

It was the common practice, where a man sold his claim to a military certificate before its issuance, for the adjutant general, on proper evidence, to issue the certificate to, and in the name of, the assignee, and land certificates made out and issued in this manner have always been considered valid; and the Commissioner of the General Land Office has, heretofore, when such certificates were located, surveyed, and returned to his department, without hesitation always issued patents in the name of the assignee. Hundreds of such certificates have been issued by a high functionary of government, running through several years, and have entered into many business transactions, passing from assignee to assignee by the various mutations of trade and speculation; and they were issued in consideration of the valuable services of a meritorious class of persons, and by them transferred for an adequate payment. But now, the assignees of such land claims, unless they have caused them to be located and patented, will, very likely, become losers. And I do not see any cause why the patents themselves should not be set aside as *void;* for, if the claim in its inception were void, no *executive* action can amend it. The reasonable conclusion is, that all *patents* for lands, issued to assignees of soldiers' certificates, which come under the prescriptions hereinafter set forth, are by law void; therefore, many persons who are holding patents, and esteeming them conclusive titles to lands, may be reckoning on empty shadows as evidences of property. In order to a better understanding of the subject, it will be necessary to state the case more fully. Formerly, any person who was entitled to a military land certificate could sell his claim, and, by delivering the evidences of his services to the purchaser, and the deed of conveyance, the transfer became complete; the latter then sent his evidences of title to the adjutant general, who thereupon issued to the purchaser, as *assignee*, a land certificate. During the summer of 1855, the adjutant general's office, together with all the archives, muniments of titles, and muster rolls, were burned and completely annihilated, not only wiping out all the record evidence of the military services which had been rendered to Texas, in the time of her necessities, but destroying what is now considered legal evidence of assignees' titles, viz., the muster-rolls on which the original claimants based their claims, and the written transfers and conveyances to assignees.

This catastrophe was and is a dire calamity to many persons, and one which the legislature, instead of endeavoring to alleviate, have, by their action, aggravated and taken advantage of, and made it a source of embarrassment to all persons having any interest in military land claims. The destruction of the military archives cannot be considered among the inevitable providences of God which, at times, afflict all nations; neither can it be considered an unavoidable accident, under common precaution; but one of gross and culpable carelessness, or, more properly, of the most criminal neglect, showing an utter disregard and contempt, by those in power, for the rights of the people. These archives were stored (not even sheltered) in an old, rickety, infirm log-hut, of contracted dimensions, such as had been built by some squatter, in the early settlement of the country; affording but questionable protection against the weather, and no security from casualties by fire, or premeditated destruction or abstraction, for purposes of fraud. While thousands upon thousands were lavished by our servants on costly furniture and gorgeous drapery, this important department of government, second to no other as a custodian of the people's rights, was consigned to a log-cabin — a hovel amid oriental public palaces.

The poorest county in the State would not trust its comparatively unimportant archives so recklessly. Now, the law establishing the Court of Claims, among other absurdities, requires a greater strictness, and is far more stringent towards military claimants, than ever was before dreamed of; and it says that all military land claims, before being patented, must be presented to the Commissioner of the Court of Claims, for examination, registry, and approval. When a military certificate is presented for said purposes, and the Commissioner has in his office *any record*, or *paper*, showing the certificate to be a genuine one, or, if the evidence of at least two credible witnesses, taken in open court, or before any officer in this State, using a seal, is produced to him, that it is a genuine one, he shall file such evidence, and shall write across the face of the certificate the word "*approved*," with the date of its approval, and sign his name thereto. "*Provided, however, that he shall withhold his approval from any bounty or donation certificate, issued* to an *assignee since* the 24*th* day of *November*, 1851, until the *genuineness* of the *assignment*, and the *identity* and *residence* of the *parties* and *witness thereto, shall be proved by at least two credible witnesses thereto.*" Now, this is most solemn mockery, or a farce: after having destroyed the evidences of the assignment, they now tell the assignee to show his original title: his rights, acquired under one law, are divested under another enactment of superior wisdom; but he is told that, if he can perform an impossibility, he may still be secured.

CHAPTER XV.

ITINERARY.

	MILES.		MILES.
Powder Horn to Lavacca	16	Goliad to Clinton	28
" Victoria	46	" Gonzales	54
" Yorktown	81	" San Antonio	90
" Sulphur Springs	121	" Helena	36
" San Antonio	151	" Refugio	28
Victoria to Quaro	40	" San Patricio	56
" Gonzales	80	" Corpus Christi, via Refugio	68
" Lockhart	110	" Brownsville Dist., via San Patricio	216
" Austin	145	" Rio Grande City	206
Powder Horn to Goliad, via Victoria	68	" Lanedo	117
Victoria to Goliad	28	Matagorda to Galveston	90
Goliad to Yorktown	22		

RIVER ROUTES FROM GALVESTON.

UP THE BRAZOS RIVER.

	MILES.		MILES.
To the mouth	60	To Waters's	16
Calvert's	3	Richmond	20
Cashe's	7	Gaston's.	22
Crosby's	4	Randon's	45
Payne's	9	San Felippe	45
Brazoria	4	Crump's	8
Columbia	12	Caney	30
Sayre's	3	Groce's	8
Tinsley's	8	Peebles's	4
Hill's	3	Lancaster	30
Towne's	2	Warren	2
Port Sillivan	60	Rock Island	40
Bolivar	1	Washington	27
Menard	3	Hidalgo	6
Lobdell's	40	Cole's	70
Manadue's	4	Munson's Shoals	40
Big Creek	2	Moseley's	25

UP THE TRINITY RIVER.

	MILES.		MILES.
To Liberty	104	To Whiterock	12
Green's Ferry	6	Carolina	5
Hardin's	22	Mrs. M'Don's	5
Robinson's	20	Evans's Gin	2
Tanner's	3	Stubblefields	8
J. Davis's	8	M'Kinzie's	6
Farrior's	12	Wright's Bluff	13
Troy	18	Cincinnati	3
Cherry's	1	Gorce's Landing	10
Bray's Camp	2	Osceola	1
Smithfield	18	Westmoreland	20
Washington's	1	Clark's Bluff	3
Drew's	4	Robbin's Ferry	10
Summers's	5	Bosman's	6
M'Cardles's	1	Cairo	10
R. Smith's	2	Alabama	16
Cochran's	6	Br'kfiel's Bluffs	20
Cedar Landing	2	Moore's Old L	2
Victory	4	Kickapoo Shoals	10
Swartwout	2	Hall's Bluff	3
Johnson's Bluff	35	Navarro	32
Harrell's Landing	10	Magnolia	31
Patrick's Ferry	15	Blackshears's	10
Jones's	4	Parker's Bluff	15
Fry's	6	West Point	10
Ryon's	4	Evans's	12
Sol Adams's	3	Pine Bluff	15

CHAPTER XVI.

GENERAL VIEW OF COAST, FACE OF COUNTRY, ISLANDS, TIMBER, HEALTH, RESOURCES, ESTACADO, MINERALS, AND RAILROADS.

THE coast of Texas, along the Gulf of Mexico, is invariably low: no high lands are to be seen, on the coast, from the Sabine to the Rio Grande: on the shore, sea-shells and flat sand-stones are to be found. The stones are scattered along the coast, from the former river to within about thirty miles east of Passo Cavallo, evidently showing, in places, at no great depth, an underlying of sand-stone rock, of a grey or yellow color. No stones are found on the coast, going west from that point, but there is black mica; and, on Del Padre's island, it is so abundant, that ship-loads taken from there would make no sensible diminution. More than three-fourths of the whole distance of sea-coast is lined with long narrow islands or peninsulas, running parallel with the main land, and forming large, irregular, and shallow bays. These lands are made by accretion, and are yearly enlarging, under ordinary circumstances; but sometimes one of the West Indian hurricanes alters their configuration. The city of Galveston is founded on one of the smallest and most unsafe of these *accretions*. They are all inhabited by small farmers and stock-raisers, and are much resorted to, in the summer months, by invalids. All kinds of fish and game are abundant. The bays so formed are the receptacles of all the rivers in Texas, excepting the Brazos and Del Norte. The back country is level, and much prairie, with timber on the river bottoms. No rock is to be found, excepting seventy or eighty miles from the coast. The rotten sand-stone is the first met: it crops out on the river bluffs. The eastern portion of the State has more favorable seasons than the country west of the Guadalupe: from thence to the Rio Grande, the want of rain is frequently the cause of a failure of crops, and to such a degree, that settlers are frequently induced to change their locations to more inland regions: in general, the farther from the seaboard, the more sure are the seasons, for the farmer. For health, the western portion of the State has always been unequalled by any part of the world — the dryness of the climate not admitting of miasmatic diseases.

The water-shed of the country is to the south-east; and, although the prairies are, to the eye, extremely level, all the main rivers are rapid.

Pine and cypress are in inexhaustible quantities, in the eastern portion of the State, on the Sabine, Neches, Trinity, San Jacinto, and their tributaries; and the lumber trade with the sea-board towns is extensive. The other kinds of timber, pretty generally diffused, are many kinds of oak, tapulo, gum, ash, peccan, hackberry, and cedar. Live-oak commences on the Brazos, and extends westwardly to the Rio Grande. The mezquit timber is west of the Guadalupe.

The richest lands in the State are between the Colorado and Brazos rivers, and on small creeks or beds of rivers not subject to overflow, such as Caney, San Bernard, and Peach Creek: on these water-courses are over 500 square miles of alluvial bottom-land, which is never, under any circumstances, subject to overflow; but this part of the State settles up slowly, as the lands are held in large tracts: the health of this region is generally good, to those who have any prudence. I have no doubt that the cattle grazing has conduced much to this effect; for, when the country was first settled, the prairie-grass and cane-bottoms were of the rankest and densest kind: now, the vegetation is kept down more by the great number of cattle and frequent fires, and the malarious influences thereby weakened. There are no minerals, on the sea-board, excepting salt, which, in the western portion, is in inexhaustible quantities. The salt region commences beyond the San Antonio; but its access to market is so obstructed, by shallow bays, that it has not been much appropriated; otherwise, could a good conveyance be had, it is the best salt region on the North American continent. Timber is scarce in that locality.

The middle portions of the State are all of an undulating description, called here *rolling prairie;* which, for beauty of scenery, are not exceeded by any State in the Union, and is considered more healthy than the planting region of the sea-board.

The north-west portion of the State, called the Prairie Estacado, and between that and the Rio Grande, including 100,000 square miles, is useless, unsettled, and will remain so for years to come: its want of water, and want of ways of access, will keep these lands for a long time out of market: they possess the qualities required for cultivation: timber is scarce in the eastern part. That portion west of the Pecos is partly timbered: this is a bold, deep stream, and empties into the Rio del Norte. This region is not less than 2500 feet above the level of the sea; and the whole will be brought into notice, and rendered valuable, if the Southern Pacific railroad be built — of which, at present, there seems to be no kind of doubt. The road is intended to run through the southern portion, from east to west; and, should it be constructed, as the ranges of mountains are north by east, and the valleys of fifty miles in width being level, such a railroad would open this almost unknown region to the uses of our people. Not one of the least of the great advantages of this important national work, would be the development of our mineral wealth: copper, silver, and coal, are known to exist, in several localities; but their value and quantity have not been ascertained. Iron of superior quality is abundant in the eastern portion of the State. Our mineralogical knowledge of the country is very circumscribed; and research should be, in some way, stimulated. No State or country in the world is more favorably situated for building railroads than Texas—the country being generally level, and, where there are inequalities in the surface, the rises and descents are generally gradual and moderate. So well adapted for common roads is it, that wheel-carriages traverse in every direction, without any regard to beaten tracks; and we have no rises, with bottomless morasses, or impassible mountain gorges; and most of the extensive surface is more like an English lawn, on a large scale, with its romantic concomitants of streamlet, dell, and slope, dotted and skirted, here and there, with its groves and forests, in primeval grandeur and luxuriance.

CHAPTER XVII.

NAMES OF DECEASED LAND CLAIMANTS.

Names of certain persons who died in Texas, in early times, and whose heirs are entitled to claims for lands — some of them to between *four and five thousand acres.* I have in my possession the evidences of hundreds of other claimants, which will, from time to time, be published.

Adams, J. M.
Allen, Layton.
Allison, Alford.
Armstrong, Wm. S.
Atwell, William.
Austin, Andrew; from New York or vicinity.
Bagly, J. S.
Baker, Stephen.
Barton, J. B.
Barton, John.
Betts, Marvin.
Bond, Burr S.
Bray, Lister J. H.
Bright, John.
Brown, William S.
Brown, W. A. J.
Buller, Bennett.
Burk, Allen.
Burk, David N.
Burknapp, Leonard; from N. Y. or Pa.
Caligrom, John.
Calk, James.
Carlisle, G. W.
Churchill, Thos. S.
Chinn, John.
Coglan, Geo. W.
Coleman, Jacob.
Comstock, Wm.
Conrad, Collin.
Conway, Matthew.
Courtman, G. F.
Crittenden, Marshall P.
Cross, John.
Cunningham, John D.
Dearick, George.
Dickinson, W.
Donal, Jôhn O.
Dubose, Wm. P. B.

Dwenny, N. J.
Dyer, George.
Edich, Henry.
Eddy, Andrew H.
Ehernberg, Herman
Ellis, Michael.
English, Robert.
Equinon, Conrad.
Fanning, John; in 1837, had a family in Texas, who left.
Fisher, J. H.
Freppard (or Treppard), Francis J.; printer, from Tenn.
Green, Wm. J.
Hamilton, James.
Harris, William.
Hasty, Henry.
Hatfield, William.
Heck, C. F.
Hitchard, John.
Hughes, Wiley.
Johnson, Charles.
Kelly, James.
Kenyon, A. D.
Kissam, P. F.
Landus, J. H.
Lloyd, Daniel; from N. Y. city.
Lynch, A. M.
Mann, William.
M'Hugh, Michael (Irish); formerly a merchant here.
M'Lellan, Alexander.
M'Murray, William.
M'Nelly, Bennett.
M'Night, George.
Numlin, John.
Oldum, Benjamin.
Paine (or Payne), George; from Clark co., Ga.
Patterson, Samuel C.
Pierce, Stephen.
Powers, J. M.
Reed, James.
Rush, Gabriel.
Ryan, Edward.
Seward, John.
Schultz, Henry.
Scott, James (sailor), was wounded in Texan army: died in New York city, in 1836: his widow, Mary Scott, was in Texas, but returned to New York, in 1838, with Captain Higgins.
Smith, Henry.
Smith, Thomas.
Stephens, William.
Stewart, Charles.
Syers, Daniel.
Taylor, Edward M.; left here, in 1838, in bad health, for New England.
Tresvunts, ———.
Volickman, J. Q.
Walters, Nicholas B.
Ward, John.
Watson, Joseph W.
Webb, James.
Wentworth, William.
Winningham, William.
Williams, T. J.
Williams, Joseph.
Winns, James C.
Witt, Hughes.
Wood, W. P.
Wrenn, Allen.
Wyatts, Peyton S.

NOTICE.

Persons claiming as heirs to any of the foregoing, or having any other legal business, in Texas, which they desire attended to, will be promptly answered by addressing me.

D. E. E. BRAMAN.

MATAGORDA CITY, *Matagorda County*, TEXAS. *Attorney and Counsellor at Law.*

REFERENCES.

Hon. James C. Wilson, Comm. Court of Claims, Austin; Hon. Stephen Crosby, Comm. General Land Office, Austin; Hon. James H. Bell, Judge First Judicial District, Brazoria; Hon. Matthew Talbot, Chief Justice, Matagorda county; Nelson, Clements, & Co., New York; Browning, Stewart, & Allen, New York.

CHAPTER XVIII.

POST-OFFICES IN TEXAS, AS FURNISHED BY THE POSTMASTER OF GALVESTON, WITH CORRECTIONS, TO DECEMBER 1, 1856.

[County towns are designated by an asterisk (*).]

POST-OFFICES.	COUNTIES.
Alma	Rusk.
Almond Grove	Red River.
Alta Springs	Limestone.
Alto	Cherokee.
Alton	Denton.
Alley's Mills	Cass.
Alum Creek	Bastrop.
Alvarado	Johnston.
Alguna	San Patricio.
Anadarco	Rusk.
Anagua	Victoria.
Anahuac	Liberty.
Anderson	Grimes.
Antioch	Lavaca.
Angelina	Angelina.
Aransas	Refugio.
Ash Springs	Harrison.
Ashton's	Shelby.
Ashville	Harrison.
Athens*	Henderson.
Austin*	Travis.
Avant	Freestone.
Bagdad	Williamson.
Black Jack Grove	Hopkins.
Black Oak	Hopkins.
Black Jack Spr's	Fayette.
Barren Ridge	Van Zandt.
Bason Springs	Grayson.
Bastrop*	Bastrop.
Bean Creek	Hunt.
Bear Creek	Sabine.
Bearsden	Lavaca.
Beaumont*	Jefferson.
Beaver	Anderson.
Bedi	Grimes.
Bellevieu	Rusk.
Bellville*	Austin.
Belmont	Gonzales.
Belone	Austin.
Belton*	Bell.
Belzora	Smith.
Bendy's Landi'g	Tyler.
Ben Franklin	Lamar.
Bethany	Panola.

POST-OFFICES.	COUNTIES.	POST-OFFICES.	COUNTIES.
Bethel............	Anderson.	Caldwell*.........	Burleson.
Berrien	Smith.	Caledonia.........	Rusk.
Benton	Harrison.	Calhoun...........	Rusk.
Bevelport.........	Jasper.	Cameron*	Milam.
Big Creek	Fort Bend.	Caney	Matagorda.
Big Dollar........	Wood.	Canton*	Van Zandt.
Billum's Creek..	Tyler.	Carizo	Webb.
Biloxi	Newton.	Carthage*........	Panola.
Birdville*	Tarrant.	Castroville*......	Medina.
Black Hill	Kauffman.	Cat Springs......	Austin.
Blossom Prairie	Lamar.	Carolina..........	Falls.
Blue Hill.........	Williamson.	Calloway	Upshur.
Blue Bluff........	M'Lellan.	Cambridge.......	Rusk.
Bluff Springs....	Travis.	Camden	Rusk.
Boerne*	Kerr.	Case's Mills......	Travis.
Bonham*.........	Fannin.	Caney Head......	Tyler.
Bonito............	Guadalupe.	Cannonville......	Comal.
Boonville*	Brazos.	Centre............	Rusk.
Boston*..........	Bowie.	Cedar Fork	Kauffman.
Bould Springs...	M'Lellan.	Cedar Bayou.....	Liberty.
Box Creek........	Cherokee.	Cedar Creek	Bastrop.
Brazos St. Jago	Cameron.	Cedar Grove.....	Kauffman.
Brazos Bottom..	Burleson.	Cedar Hill	Dallas.
Brazoria*	Brazoria.	Cedar Lake......	Brazoria.
Brackett..........	Kinney.	Centreville*......	Leon.
Brenham*........	Washington.	Chambersia	Liberty.
Bright Star......	Hopkins.	Chambersville...	Liberty.
Brownsboro'.....	Henderson.	Charco	Goliad.
Brownsville*....	Cameron.	Chambers's Cr'k	Ellis.
Buena Vista.....	Shelby.	Chance's Prairie	Burleson.
Buffalo............	Henderson.	Chappel Hill.....	Washington.
Bunker Hill......	Rusk.	Chermo	Nacogdoches.
Burkville*	Newton.	China Grove.....	Gonzales.
Burleson	Lampasas.	Cincinnati........	Walker.
Burnet*	Burnet.	Clayton	Grayson.
Butler............	Freestone.	Clarksville*......	Red River
Bryant's Station	Milam.	Clear Fork	Caldwell.

POST-OFFICES.	COUNTIES.
Clear Creek......	Denton.
Clinton...........	Dewitt.
Clopton...........	Smith.
Coffeeville	Upshur.
Cold Springs.....	Polk.
Coletto	Dewitt.
Colita..............	Polk.
College Mound..	Kauffman.
Columbia	Brazoria.
Columbus*	Colorado.
Comanche Peak	Johnson.
Concord...........	Harrison.
Concrete..........	Dewitt.
Copano............	Refugio.
Corpus Christi*	Neuces.
Corsicana*	Navarro.
Cotland............	Newton.
Cotton Gin.......	Freestone.
Cotton Plant.....	Rusk.
Covington........	Hill.
Crockett*........	Houston.
Crimea............	Hill.
Cusseta...........	Cass.
Cuero*............	Dewitt.
Cunningham's ..	Bastrop.
Cypress City.....	Harris.
Dangerfield	Titus.
Dallas*......... ...	Dallas.
Danville...........	Montgomery.
Deer Creek	Falls.
De Kalb	Bowie.
Dhanis............	Medina.
Douglass..........	Nacogdoches.
Douglassville....	Cass.
Durk Creek......	Dallas.
Dresden	Navarro.
Duncan's Wood..	Orange.
Eagle Lake	Colorado.
Eagle Pass*......	Kinney.
Earpville	Upshur.
Edinburgh	Cameron.
Egypt.............	Colorado.
Elkhart..	Anderson.
Elm Creek	Falls.
El Paso*..........	El Paso.
Elwood*	Madison.
Elysian Fields...	Harrison.
Eutaw	Robertson.
Erin	Jasper.
Fairfield	Freestone.
Fairmount........	Sabine.
Fair Play.........	Panola.
Farmer's Bran'h	Dallas.
Fayetteville......	Fayette.
Furguson	Grayson.
Fincastle	Henderson.
Flintham's T'n'd	Red River.
Flora	Smith.
Flowerdale	Freestone.
Forrest Home...	Cass.
Fort Graham....	Hill.
Fort Worth	Tarrant.
Fort Belknap*..	Young.
Fort Inge.........	Uvalde.
Four Mile Prai'e	Van Zandt.
Fredericksburg.	Gillespie.
Fredonia.........	Rusk.
Freedom	Harrison.
Frelsburg.........	Colorado.
Friendship.......	Harrison.
Gainsville.........	Cook.
Gallatia	Harrison.
Galveston.........	Galveston.
Garden Valley...	Smith.

POST-OFFICES.	COUNTIES.
Garcita	Victoria.
Gay Hill	Washington.
Georgetown	Williamson.
Gilbert	M'Lellan.
Gilmer	Upshur.
Gilliland Creek	Travis.
Gold Hill	Hopkins.
Goliad	Goliad.
Gonzales	Gonzales.
Gouldsboro'	Titus.
Goshen	Walker.
Glade Springs	Harrison.
Graham's Mills	Shelby.
Grand Bluff	Panola.
Grand Cape	Liberty.
Gray Rock	Titus.
Greenville	Hunt.
Grimesville	Grimes.
Gulf Prairie	Brazoria.
Gum Spring	Smith.
Halifax	Polk.
Hallettsville	Lavaca.
Hall's Bluff	Houston.
Hamburg	Van Zandt.
Hamilton	Shelby.
Harmony Hill	Rusk.
Harrington	Angelina.
Harrisburg	Harris.
Hartville	Austin.
Hackberry Gro'e	Grayson.
Havanna	Dallas.
Helena*	Karnes.
Henderson*	Rusk.
Hendersonville	Anderson.
Hesterville	Dewitt.
Hickory Hill	Cass.
Highland	Collin.
Hilliard's	Shelby.
Hillsboro'	Hill.
Hickory Grove	Smith.
Hodge's Bend	Fort Bend.
Holly Springs	Wood.
Home	Walker.
Honey Grove	Fannin.
Hooker's	Hunt.
Hopewell	Upshur.
Hopkinsville	Gonzales.
Hortensville	Karnes.
Houseville	Harris.
Houston*	Harris.
Howard	Bell.
Huntsville*	Walker.
Hornsby	———.
Independence	Washington.
Indian Grove	Grayson.
Indianola	Calhoun.
Industry	Austin.
Ioni	Anderson.
Jacksonville	Cherokee.
Jamestown	Smith.
Jasper*	Jasper.
Jefferson	Cass.
Johns's	Liberty.
Johnson's Stat'n	Tarrant.
Jonesville	Harrison.
Jordan's Salines	Van Zandt.
Jackson	Mason.
Jena	Falls.
Kauffman	Kauffman.
Keechi	Freestone.
Kentucky Town	Grayson.
Kemp	Kauffman.
Kerrsville	Kerr.
Kickapoo	Anderson.

POST-OFFICES.	COUNTIES.
Kidd's Mills.....	Leon.
Kinlock..........	Panola.
Kiomatia	Red River.
Knoxville.........	Cherokee.
Lagrange.........	Fayette.
Lake	Trinity.
Lake Creek......	Lamar.
Lamar............	Refugio.
Lampassas*.....	Lampassas.
Lancaster.........	Dallas.
Laredo*..........	Webb.
Larissa...........	Cherokee.
Locust Shade....	Dallas.
Llano	Llano.
Leona............	Leon.
Lexington	Burleson.
Liberty*..........	Liberty.
Liberty Hill......	Williamson.
Licke..............	Fannin.
Linden*..........	Cass.
Lineville..........	Panola.
Linflat............	Nacogdoches.
Linwood.........	Cherokee.
Little Elm........	Denton.
Live Oak.........	Dewitt.
Liverpool.........	Brazoria.
Livingston*......	Polk.
Lockhart*........	Caldwell.
Lone Star.........	Titus.
Long Point.......	Washington.
Lynchburg	Harris.
Lyons.............	Fayette.
Lewisville........	Denton.
M'Goffinsville....	El Paso.
M'Gee's..........	Liberty.
M'Kinney*......	Collin.
M'Millan's.......	Panola.
Madisonville*...	Madison.
Madison..........	Orange.
Magnolia.........	Anderson.
Magnolia Spri'gs	Jasper.
Malakoff	Henderson.
Maple Springs...	Red River.
Marion*	Angelina.
Marlin*..........	Falls.
Marlow's Mills..	Anderson.
Marshall..........	Harrison.
Matagorda*.....	Matagorda.
Mayesville........	Bexar.
Melrose..........	Nacogdoches.
Meridian*.......	Bosque.
Merilltown	Travis.
Meyerville.......	Dewitt.
Midway..........	Madison.
Middletown......	Goliad.
Milam*..........	Sabine.
Milford..	Ellis.
Millhein..........	Austin.
Mill Creek........	Bowie.
Millican's.........	Brazos.
Millville..........	Rusk.
Millwood.........	Collin.
Mission Valley..	Victoria.
Mitchell's........	Walker.
Monterey.........	Red River.
Montgomery*...	Montgomery.
Moore's...........	Bowie.
Morales de L'v'ca	Jackson.
Moscow..........	Polk.
Moulton...........	Gonzales.
Mt. Carmel......	Smith.
Mt. Enterprise..	Rusk.
Mt. Petria........	Dewitt.
Mt. Pleasant*...	Titus.

POST-OFFICES.	COUNTIES.	POST-OFFICES.	COUNTIES.
Mt. Vernon......	Limestone.	Personville	Limestone.
Mound Prairie..	Anderson.	Perry	M'Lellan.
Mud Springs....	Denton.	Perryville	Bastrop.
Mulberry Grove	Grayson.	Petersburg	Lavaca.
Murvall	Rusk.	Pierpont Place..	Dewitt.
Muskeet..........	Navarro.	Pilot Grove	Grayson.
Mustang	Lavaca.	Pilot Point.......	Denton.
Myrtle Springs..	Bowie.	Pine Bluff........	Red River.
Naches............	Houston.	Pine Hill	Rusk.
Nacogdoches*...	Nacogdoches.	Pine Island	Jefferson.
Nashville	Milam.	Pinetown.........	Cherokee.
Navarro	Leon.	Pinetree	Upshur.
Navasoto	Grimes.	Pin Oak...........	Fayette.
New Braunfels*	Comal.	Piano	Collin.
New Danville....	Rusk.	Pleasant Hill....	Hopkins.
Newburg Mills..	Parker.	Pleasant Run....	Dallas.
Newport..........	Walker.	Plenitude	Anderson.
New Salem.......	Rusk.	Plum Creek......	Caldwell.
Newton*	Newton.	Plum Grove......	Fayette.
New Ulm.........	Austin.	Point Isabel......	Cameron.
North Sulphur..	Fannin.	Point Monterey..	Cass.
Neucestown......	Neuces.	Point Pleasant...	Upshur.
Oak Grove	Titus.	Pond Springs....	Williamson.
Oakland..........	Lavaca.	Post Oak Island	Williamson.
Oat Meal.........	Burnet.	Porter's Prairie	Burleson.
Odessa	Wise.	Port Caddo......	Harrison.
Ogsburn	Smith.	Port Lavaca......	Calhoun.
Omega	Upshur.	Port Sillivan.....	Milam.
Owensville*......	Robertson.	Post Oak..........	Bexar.
Orizaba	———.	Powellton.........	Harrison.
Palestine*........	Anderson.	Prairie Creek....	Dallas.
Pallace Hill	Dallas.	Prairie Cottage..	Colorado.
Pamplin's Creek	Tyler.	Prairie Lea	Caldwell.
Paulineville	Tyler.	Prairie Mount...	Lamar.
Parker's Bluff...	Navarro.	Prairie Plains...	Grimes.
Paris*	Lamar.	Prairieville.......	Kauffman.
Peachtree Vill'ge	Tyler.	Preston	Wharton.

POST-OFFICES.	COUNTIES.
Price's Creek....	Dewitt.
Prospect	Burleson.
Prosperity........	Falls.
Providence Hill.	Tyler.
Porter's Bluff...	Navarro.
Pulaski...........	Panola.
Panamaria	Karnes.
Pine Grove.......	Austin.
Pecan Grove.....	Gonzales.
Peoria	Hill.
Palo Alto	Gonzales.
Quihi	Medina.
Quintana	Brazoria.
Quitman*	Wood.
Rancho	Gonzales.
Red Oak	Ellis.
Red Rock.........	Upshur.
Red Springs.....	———.
Red Top..........	Harrison.
Reed's Settlem't	Panola.
Reedyville........	Hidalgo.
Refugio*	Refugio.
Retina	Hopkins.
Retreat	Grimes.
Richland Cross'g	Navarro.
Richmond*	Fort Bend
Rio Grande C'y*	Starr.
Roadville	Anderson.
Rock Island......	Austin.
Rock Hill.........	Collin.
Rocky Mills......	Lavaca.
Rockwall	Kauffman.
Roma..............	Starr.
Rose Hill.	Harris.
Roseland	Collin.
Round Top.......	Fayette.
Round Prairie...	Lamar.
Rusk*.............	Cherokee.
Rutersville	Fayette.
Rutherford.......	Parker.
Round Rock.....	Williamson.
Robertson	Hill.
Robins's Ferry..	Houston.
Sabine City......	Jefferson.
Sabine Town	Sabine.
Sabinal............	Uvalde.
Salado.............	Bell.
Salem	Newton.
Saluria	Calhoun.
Salt Stream......	Gonzales.
San Antonio* ...	Bexar.
San Andres	Milam.
San Augustine*	San Augustine.
San Bernard.....	Colorado.
San Cosma	Rusk.
San Felipe	Austin.
Sand Fly	Bastrop.
San Gabriel......	Williamson.
Sand Hill.........	Rusk.
San Marcos*....	Hays.
San Patricio*...	San Patricio.
San Pedro........	Houston.
Sandy Point.....	Brazoria.
San Saba*.......	San Saba.
Savannah.........	Red River.
Sebastopol.......	———.
Seguin*...........	Guadalupe.
Selma	Bexar.
Sempronius	Austin.
Seven Leagues..	Smith.
Seven Oaks	Galveston.
Scyene	Dallas.
Shannon's........	Montgomery.
Shelby	Austin.

POST-OFFICES.	COUNTIES.
Shelbyville*.....	Shelby.
Sherman.........	Grayson.
Shiloh	Hunt.
Shockey's Prai'e	Lamar.
Sisterdale........	Comal.
Smithfield	Polk.
Smithland........	Cass.
Skull Creek......	Colorado.
Springfield	Limestone.
Spring Hill......	Navarro.
Sugar Hill.......	Panola.
Sulphur Bluff...	Hopkins.
Sulphur Springs	Cherokee.
Summer Grove..	Smith.
Sumpter*........	Trinity.
Sutherland Spr's	Bexar.
Swartwout.......	Liberty.
Swearengen's....	Austin.
Sweet Home.....	Lavaca.
Tehuacana Spr's	Limestone.
Taos	Navarro.
Tarkington's P'e	Liberty.
Tarrant*	Hopkins.
Taylorsville*....	Wise.
Telico	Ellis.
Tenn'e Colony...	Anderson.
Texana*	Jackson.
Timber Creek...	Hunt.
Town Bluff.......	Tyler.
Travis	Austin.
Trinidad	Kauffman.
Troupe...........	Smith.
Troutman........	Cherokee.
Troy	Freestone.
Truet's Store....	Shelby
Tyler*	Smith.
Triar..............	Bexar.
Union Bridge....	Titus.
Union Hill.......	Washington.
Unionville.......	Cass.
Uvalde*..........	Uvalde.
Valley............	Guadalupe.
Victoria*	Victoria.
Vine Grove.......	Washington.
Waco Village*..	M'Lellan.
Walling's Ferry.	Rusk.
Walnut Hill......	Panola.
Wardville.........	Johnston.
Warren...........	Fannin.
Warsaw Prairie.	Kauffman.
Washington*....	Washington.
Waverly..........	Walker.
Waxahachie*....	Ellis.
Weatherford*...	Parker.
Webberville......	Travis.
Weiss Bluff.......	Jasper.
West Liberty....	Liberty.
Weston...........	Collin.
Wharton*........	Wharton.
Wheelock.........	Robertson.
White Cottage...	Shelby.
White Oak.......	Hopkins.
White Rock......	Hill.
Willow Springs..	Milam.
Winnsboro'.......	Wood.
Woods's	Panola.
Woodland.........	Hopkins.
Woodville.........	Tyler.
Woodboro'.......	Grayson.
Young's Settle't	Bastrop.
Zavalia...........	Jasper.
Zoar	Gonzales.

CHAPTER XIX.

COUNTIES AND COUNTY SITES.

[County towns not established are designated by an asterisk (*).]

COUNTIES.	COUNTY-TOWNS.
Anderson	Palestine.
Angelina	Marion.
Austin	San Felipe.
Atascosa	Newtown.
Bastrop	Bastrop.
Bell	Belton.
Burnet	Hamilton.
Bexar	San Antonio
Bowie	Boston.
Brazoria	Brazoria.
Brazos	Booneville.
Burleson	Caldwell.
Bosque	Meridian.
Bandera*	———.
Brown*	———.
Caldwell	Lockhart.
Calhoun	Indianola.
Cameron	Brownsville.
Cass	Linden.
Cherokee	Rusk.
Collin	M'Kinney.
Colorado	Columbus.
Comal	New Braunfels.
Cook	Gainsville.
Coryell	Gatesville.
Comanche*	———.
Dallas	Dallas.
Denton	Alton.
Dewitt	Clinton.
Ellis	Waxahachi.
El Paso	San Eleazario.
Erath	Stephensville.
Falls	Marlin.
Fannin	Bonham.
Fayette	Lagrange.
Fort Bend	Richmond.
Freestone	Fairfield.
Galveston	Galveston.
Gillespie	Fredericksburg.
Goliad	Goliad.
Gonzales	Gonzales.
Grayson	Sherman.
Grimes	Anderson.
Guadalupe	Seguin.
Harris	Houston.
Hidalgo	Edinburgh.
Harrison	Marshall.
Hays	San Marcos.
Hill	Hillsboro'.
Henderson	Athens.
Hopkins	Tarrant.
Houston	Crockett.

COUNTIES.	COUNTY-TOWNS.	COUNTIES.	COUNTY-TOWNS.
Hunt	Greenville.	Presidio	Presidio C. H.
Jackson	Texana.	Parker	Weatherford.
Johnson	Wardville.	Palo Pinto	Golconda.
Jasper	Jasper.	Red River	Clarksville.
Jefferson	Beaumont.	Refugio	Refugio.
Jack	Mesquiteville.	Rusk	Henderson.
Kauffman	Kauffman.	Robertson	Owensville.
Kinney	Brackett.	Sabine	Milam.
Kerr	Kerrsville.	San Augustine	San Augustine.
Lamar	Paris.	San Patricio	San Patricio.
Lavaca	Hallettsville.	Shelby	Shelbyville.
Leon	Centreville.	Smith	Tyler.
Liberty	Liberty.	Starr	Rio Grande City.
Limestone	Springfield.	San Saba	Rochester.
Lampasas	Lampasas.	Tarrant	Birdville.
Live Oak*	———.	Titus	Mt. Pleasant.
Llano	Llano.	Travis	Austin.
Matagorda	Matagorda.	Trinity	Sumpter.
M'Lennan	Waco.	Tyler	Woodville.
Medina	Castroville.	Upshur	Gilmer.
Milam	Cameron.	Uvalde	Uvalde.
Montgomery	Montgomery	Van Zandt	Canton.
Maverick	Eagle Pass.	Victoria	Victoria.
M'Culloch	———.	Walker	Huntsville.
Nacogdoches	Nacogdoches.	Washington	Brenham.
Navarro	Corsicana.	Webb	Webb C. H.
Newton	Newton.	Wharton	Wharton.
Neuces	Corpus Christi.	Williamson	Georgetown.
Orange	Madison.	Wood	Quitman.
Panola	Carthage.	Wise*	———.
Polk	Livingston.	Young	Belknap.

CHAPTER XX.

MISCELLANEOUS.

Elevations of different Points in Texas: mostly from De Cordova and Fraser's "Traveller's Guide."

	FEET.		FEET.
Lavaca	24	Llano Estacado..... 2300 to	2500
Matagorda	12	Guadalupe, m. of Sandies	50
Cibolo	350	San Antonio	635
Castroville	767	Fort Inge	835
Leona mt. (near Ft. Inge)	950	R. San Pedro, first cross'g	859
Rio San Pedro, last cross'g	1827	Table-lands of Texas	2091
Howard's Springs	2075	High table-land beyond	3008
Live Oak Creek	2337	Rio Pecos Valley	2658
Rio Escondido, first cross'g	3950	Leon Spring	4240
Highest point; road to El Paso	5896	Painted Camp	5020
Eagle Spring	4842	Providence Creek	5492
El Paso	3750	First point on Rio Grande	3700
Big Witchita	900	Mouth of Little Witchita	750
Head of main or S. F. of Red River	2450	Junction of the S. and N. Forks of Red River	1100

The general average of the islands and peninsulas, along the coast, is not more than five or six feet above sea level.

United States Military Stations.

Ringgold Barr's,	Starr county.	Fort Mar'n Scott,	Gillespie county.
Fort M'Intosh...	Webb "	" Mason......	Bexar "
" Brown	Maverick "	" Croughan..	Burnet "
" Clarke......	Kinney "	" Phan'm Hill,	Bosque "
" Davis.......	Presidio "	" Graham....	Hill "
" Leighton ..	on the R. Grande.	" Worth......	W. F. of Trinity.
" Bliss.........	El Paso "	San Antonio.....	Bexar "
" Merrill......	Live Oak "	Camp Cooper....	" "
" Inge.........	Uvalde "	Camanche Age'y (Tex. Gov.)..	Cook "
" Ferrell......	Bexar "	Caddo Agency (Tex. Gov.)..	Young "
" M'Kavit ...	" "		
" Chadbourne	" "		

Mexican Land Measure.

In all lands granted by Spain and Mexico, the quantities are designated by *leagues*, *labors*, and *varas*, and their fractions. We have, therefore, reduced them to English measure, as follows, viz.:

One vara is equal to 33⅓ inches: 5646 square varas, one acre, equal to 4840 square yards. One labor is 1,000,000 square varas, equal to $177\frac{136}{1000}$ acres. One-third league is 8,333·333 square varas, equal to 1476 acres. One league is 25,000,000 square varas, equal to 4428 acres. One league and one labor is 26,000,000 square varas, equal to 4605 acres.

To find the number of acres in a given number of square varas, divide by 5646.

To bring English measure into Mexican, add eight per cent.

CHAPTER XXI.

STATISTICS: FROM RICHARDSON'S "TEXAS ALMANAC," PUBLISHED BY THE "GALVESTON NEWS."

NEGROES, HORSES, AND CATTLE, IN 1850 AND 1855.

COUNTIES.	NEGROES.			HORSES.			CATTLE.		
	1850.	1855.	Incr'se in five years.	1850.	1855.	Incr'se in five years.	1850.	1855	Incr'se in five years.
Anderson	600	1917	1317	943	1721	778	7621	13350	5729
Angelina	196	291	95	558	569	11	6371	9196	2825
Austin	1549	2353	804	2715	3447	732	22550	33019	10469
Bastrop	919	1748	829	1912	3031	1119	18610	25592	6982
Bell	......	466	......	......	2119	......	......	16607	......
Bosque	......	34	......	......	361	......	......	1402	......
Bexar	389	980	591	704	3791	3087	9289	40272	30983
Bowie	1641	1866	225	1349	1089	260	8184	5153	3031
Brazoria	3507	4294	787	2454	4576	2122	50192	53671	3479
Brazos	148	427	279	448	754	306	6309	13762	7453
Burleson	500	1054	554	973	1860	887	12766	26009	13243
Burnet	......	150	.....	......	703	......	......	9021	......
Caldwell	274	1171	879	218	4113	3895	4042	19238	15196
Calhoun	234	352	118	410	1131	721	8278	21089	12811
Cameron	53	15	38	942	3884	2942	4319	13424	9105
Cass	1902	3518	1616	1340	2010	670	8157	7297	890
Cherokee	1283	2286	1003	1618	1265	353	9583	4128	5455
Collin	134	438	304	977	2316	1339	4813	11098	6285
Colorado	723	1580	857	3107	1869	1238	22261	13458	8803
Comal	61	126	65	119	948	829	1283	10590	9307
Cooke	1	123	122	68	400	332	503	4328	3825
Coryell	......	139	......	......	789	......	......	4242	......
Dallas	207	481	274	756	2642	1868	3643	13192	9549
Denton	10	79	69	249	926	677	1754	8389	6635
Dewitt	568	963	395	2635	5928	3293	17954	31518	13564
Ellis	77	517	440	327	1593	1266	2858	13852	10994
El Paso	......	......	......	......	429	......	......	2216	......
Falls	......	851	......	......	1664	......	......	14197	......
Fannin	528	1019	491	1877	2085	208	10192	12688	2496
Fayette	1016	2072	1056	1722	4397	2675	14085	26952	12867
Fort Bend	1554	1746	192	1835	2898	1063	29223	30380	1157
Freestone	......	2167	......	......	1672	......	......	13279	......
Galveston	714	963	249	391	831	440	13328	15600	2272
Gillespie	5	63	58	86	512	426	788	10190	9402
Goliad	213	416	203	432	1962	1530	7731	18733	11002
Gonzales	601	2140	1539	2319	5422	3103	29726	38231	8505
Grayson	186	602	416	873	2283	1410	5111	13566	8455
Grimes	1680	3177	1497	1570	2538	968	22324	18915	3409
Guadalupe	335	1637	1302	1389	3646	2257	11563	26280	14717
Harris	905	1195	290	1718	2264	546	29123	45106	15983
Harrison	6213	7014	801	2940	2783	157	12530	7493	5037
Hays	128	517	389	216	1029	818	1733	4526	2793
Henderson	81	411	330	264	415	151	3392	3817	425

NEGROES, HORSES, AND CATTLE, IN 1850 AND 1855.

COUNTIES.	NEGROES.			HORSES.			CATTLE.		
	1850.	1855.	Incr'se in five years.	1850.	1855.	Incr'se in five years.	1850.	1855.	Incr'se in five years.
Hill	......	254	......	......	887	......	......	9156	......
Hidalgo	......	......	......	......	109	......	......	670	......
Hopkins	154	352	198	850	1870	1020	8963	18248	9285
Houston	673	1595	992	1028	1501	473	13016	12949	67
Hunt	41	198	157	361	1838	1477	3480	17871	14391
Jackson	339	717	378	1074	1451	377	20792	40437	19715
Jasper	541	991	450	437	613	176	5800	6127	327
Jefferson	269	216	35	1927	2785	858	29159	39657	10498
Johnson	......	120	......	......	591	......	......	5047	......
Karnes	......	......	......	......	......	......	......	......	......
Kauffman	65	329	264	303	1122	819	2865	11308	8443
Kinney	......	......	......	......	......	......	......	......	......
Lamar	1085	1296	211	1988	2487	499	14483	12592	1891
Lavaca	432	1004	572	1456	2107	652	12590	16228	3638
Leon	621	1455	834	1202	1901	699	14089	14533	444
Liberty	892	922	30	2451	3203	752	45670	58031	12361
Limestone	618	680	62	1248	1799	551	13294	21360	8066
M'Lennan	......	1048	......	......	1887	......	......	15003	......
Madison	......	429	......	......	1190	......	......	10436	......
Matagorda	1208	1578	371	1078	1638	560	35009	33334	1675
Medina	28	25	3	90	300	210	797	5778	4981
Milam	436	749	313	1151	2565	1414	10630	18185	7555
Montgomery	945	1448	503	1006	1037	21	11777	6325	5452
Nacogdoches	1404	1714	310	1486	2378	892	9879	14572	4693
Navarro	246	1135	889	896	2812	1916	9265	29505	20240
Newton	426	602	176	331	496	165	4940	4481	459
Neuces	47	89	42	677	1315	638	10075	14364	4289
Orange	......	......	......	......	......	......	......	......	......
Panola	1193	1990	797	1116	1531	415	6719	8633	1914
Polk	805	1450	645	1058	1037	21	15436	5408	10028
Presidio	......	......	......	......	......	......	......	......	......
Red River	1406	1807	401	1343	1731	388	9182	12811	3629
Refugio	19	148	129	407	1550	1143	10124	14833	4709
Robertson	264	1239	975	710	1584	874	11634	19959	8325
Rusk	2136	3620	1484	2480	2712	232	12423	9670	2753
Sabine	942	800	142	784	247	537	7293	2144	5149
San Augustine	1561	1448	113	1048	946	102	9063	6003	3060
San Patricio	3	21	18	47	252	205	1692	10510	8818
Shelby	961	775	186	1353	941	412	10985	7172	3713
Smith	717	2439	1722	980	1684	704	6133	5557	576
Starr	......	......	......	......	......	......	......	......	......
Tarrant	65	280	215	159	1696	1537	1549	13570	12021
Titus	467	1216	749	953	1053	100	6838	7160	322
Travis	791	2068	1277	1511	3746	2235	11953	18396	6443
Trinity	......	260	......	......	516	......	......	7017	......
Tyler	418	752	334	547	713	166	4938	5484	546
Upshur	682	1784	1102	996	1025	29	5473	3026	2447
Uvalde	......	......	......	......	......	......	......	......	......
Van Zandt	40	125	85	623	643	20	4097	7520	3423
Victoria	571	861	290	1838	2988	1150	13288	28243	14955
Walker	1301	2765	1464	1818	1930	112	23923	11947	11976
Washington	2817	4399	1582	2552	4408	1856	21873	22090	217
Webb	......	......	......	......	274	......	......	3539	......
Wharton	1242	1798	556	1173	2179	1006	15668	14977	691
Williamson	155	757	602	2223	4045	1822	21060	21832	772
Wood	......	354	......	......	537	......	......	4069	......

It will be seen that the slave population has increased from 58,161, in 1850, to 105,704, in 1855. But the number of slaves assessed, in 1850, was only 49,197—showing an increase, by the assessments of 1855, of more than 100 per cent. The ad valorem value has risen from $361, in 1850, to $505, in 1855. Six counties show a decrease in slaves, during the five years. Two, Cameron and Medina, are on the Rio Grande; and the decrease arises from their proximity to Mexico, making this kind of property a very uncertain one. The other four counties are in Eastern Texas; and the decrease arises, probably, from emigration to the counties further west. Those counties which, in the column of 1850, are blank, have been organized since that time; and those in the column of 1855 that are blank, are not yet organized; at least, three of them have not been, and from the other two no returns have been made.

Horses have increased from 89,223, in 1850, to 177,444, in 1855, or nearly 100 per cent. Eight counties, seven of which are in the eastern portion of the State, show a decrease in this stock, during the five years. This arises from the want of grass in Eastern Texas, the horses having been removed to the western prairies. To the same cause is to be attributed the decrease of cattle which occurs in twenty counties of the State; all in the eastern counties, except Colorado. The decrease in these twenty counties has taken place in the face of an increase in the State of more than 100 per cent., during the five years. This, alone, is sufficient to establish the truth of what we have elsewhere stated, in regard to the great superiority of the western counties for stock-raising. A careful perusal of the foregoing table will show the very rapid increase, in this kind of stock, since 1850. In Bexar county, alone, the increase of cattle was from 9289 head to 40,272, or about 450 per cent., during the five years.

The whole number of horses and cattle assessed, in 1850, was 750,352,* valued at $5,222,270; whilst, in 1855, the number had

* The Census Report for 1850 gives the whole number of horses and cattle at 1,019,337, while the assessment for the same year returned only 750,352, making a difference of 268,985 head. We cannot conceive why so large a difference should occur; for, admitting that the Census Report is an over-estimate, and the assessment below the actual number, there is still too great a difference to reconcile by any ordinary allowance for error. There is no doubt but that the assessed number is, annually, considerably below the true one.

risen to 1,603,146, valued at $16,916,833, or an increase of about 110 per cent. in number, and of more than 300 per cent. in value.

The above statement shows a most astonishing result, considering that only twenty years have passed since Texas was, literally, an uncultivated waste. Ten years have now elapsed since the annexation of Texas to the United States, during which time her wealth has increased nearly five-fold. It will be seen that the land assessed has increased from 31,967,480 acres to 45,419,836, and in value from $17,776,101 to $58,334,624, or more than 300 per cent., during the ten years. The average value per acre has risen from about 55 cents, in 1846, to $1·28, in 1855, or more than 230 per cent.

Negroes have increased in number from 31,099, valued at $10,142,198, or an average value of $324 per head, to 105,704, valued at $53,422,663, or an average value per head of $505. This gives an increase in number of a little more than 300 per cent., and in value of more than 500 per cent.

The whole number of horses and cattle, in 1846, was but 411,100; since which time they have increased to 1,603,146, or 400 per cent. The increase in value has been still greater, having risen from $2,929,372, in 1846, to $16,916,833, in 1855, or nearly 600 per cent. Under the head of money at interest, goods in store, etc., is included also miscellaneous property, and the value of town lots. It will be seen that the increase in the value of the whole has been from $3,543,501 to $20,649,024, or nearly 600 per cent. The average increase of all kinds of property, during the ten years, as exhibited in the column of aggregate taxable property, will be found to be about 430 per cent., having risen, in the aggregate value, from $34,391,174 to about $150,000,000.

CHAPTER XXII.

REMARKS ON PRESENT AND FUTURE PROSPECTS.

It will be seen, by the foregoing tables, that Texas has progressed, in substantial wealth, in a rapid ratio, notwithstanding the many adverse circumstances under which she labors; the most material of which are, difficulty of access, and lack of railroads, or other good communications to the interior. But emigrants, with willing minds and ready hands, are all the appliances needed for bringing these things about, and making her the *superior* producing and exporting State of our glorious Confederacy. This is a country where the rich, the poor, and those who have a modicum of this world's goods, may find soil, climate, and productions suited to their various wants; and never, in any other country, did such a combination of happy circumstances concur to make man satisfied with his earthly lot. The wide-spread and luxuriant prairies, and the rich alluvial loams, invite honest industry to come, till, and reap the abundant rewards of harvest.

The high wall of despotism with which Spain and Mexico surrounded this country, and, for a long time, excluded it from the progressive influences of the world, has been thrown down by Anglo-Saxon valor; the vulture and viper of tyrannic misrule have fled before the American eagle; and the degrading oppression formerly exercised by unbridled power, through its willing instruments, *Mother Church* and the military, has given way to the civic rule of benign republicanism.

When we look on Texas, and then turn our eyes to the adjacent country, Mexico, we are astonished at the contrast, so unfavorable to the latter. While she is old in theories, crimes, and civilization, with but the moral stamina and vigor of an ancient debauchee, Texas, her dismembered province, becomes, under another influence, vigorous and thrifty, with well-founded hopes of future greatness. We say to ourselves, notwithstanding it is unchristian to covet our neighbor's goods, still, where that neighbor is so improvident with the bounties which God hath bestowed, and so little thoughtful of the Giver, that the world would be much benefited with a more thrifty tenant, and no one could be injured by the change.

Nations, as well as individuals, are obligated to certain proprieties of deportment, not only among themselves, but towards others. It is true, in theory, that one sovereign nation is independent of all others; but, in practice, every civilized nation is dependent on every other; and the bad government and vicious polity of a *degraded* nation, without violating any international law, vibrate throughout the world, and demoralize all peoples.

THE END.

www.ingramcontent.com/pod-product-compliance
Lightning Source LLC
LaVergne TN
LVHW011221110826
845150LV00006B/1499

* 9 7 8 1 4 2 5 5 1 5 4 3 0 *